© Roho Publishing. All rights reserved. Printed in the United States.

ISBN: 978-1-945469-01-5

Cover Design: Jenna Stanbrough

Book Layout: Jenna Stanbrough

Roho Publishing
4040 Graphic Arts Rd
Emporia, Kansas 66801

www.rohopublishing.com

About Roho Publishing

When Kip Keino defeated Jim Ryun in the 1968 Olympic Games at 1500 meters he credited the win to "Roho." Roho is the Swahili word for spirit demonstrated through extraordinary strength and courage. The type of courage and strength that can be summoned up from deep within that will allow you to meet your goals and overcome the challenges in life. Roho Publishing focuses on the spirit of sport and is designed to inspire, encourage, motivate and teach valuable life lessons.

Dedication

My daughter, Jenna, has applied her creative abilities in editing, designing and creating the final product in this book as well as all of the other Roho Publishing books.

My family has supported and encouraged me to follow my passion in teaching, coaching, and as an athlete.

I would also like to thank the athletes whom I have had the privilege to coach over the years. With these athletes I have "practiced" many of the mental drills in this book and hopefully developed mental skills that not only improved athletic performance, but also improved each one as a person. Each of these individuals has taught me much about the qualities to be successful in life – good character, integrity, a strong work ethic, dedication and perseverance.

Preface

The *Mental Skill and Drills Athlete Workbook* goes hand in hand with the *Mental Skills and Drills for Athletes* book. It contains only the activities as a quick, easy to understand, and complete tool that can be distributed to athletes. Athletes and coaches can put what they have learned to work by completing the drills and activities in this workbook. The mental part of performance is a skill, and therefore should be trained similar to the physical part, with mental drills to improve mental skills. By learning and implementing mental skills with a systematic program, athletes and coaches will be embarking upon a rewarding journey to improve mental skills and make a positive difference.

I love the feeling of movement and the self-satisfaction from participation in a challenge. From my earliest experiences competing at the county fair, through high school and collegiate sports, I have used the concepts of sports psychology. However, initially, I had no idea I was using sports psychology.

The potato races at the county fair were fun! To balance your potato on a spoon and run as fast as you can, periodically stopping to put the potato back on the spoon was a simple but encouraging introduction to my beginning sports experiences. Not only was it enjoyable, but being able to finish ahead of the pack gave me confidence.

When I competed on the 6th, 7th, and 8th grade track and field teams, the varsity was determined by weight limit. My 6th and 7th grade years, I fell below the 90-pound limit and was junior varsity. At the beginning of my 8th grade track season, I was excited I had beefed up and broken the 90-pound barrier and expected to make varsity. However, to my dismay, they moved the weight limit to 100 pounds and I remained junior varsity. As a junior varsity competitor, I excelled in many events and that was the start of my track and field career.

In high school, I continued to work hard and grow in confidence. By my senior year, I was undefeated at my specialty, the 800-meter run, and entered the state meet with a goal of winning. But the unexpected happened. At the beginning of the final lap, I was tripped and fell down. When I got up, my competitors were far up the track. I took off sprinting and caught them all by the beginning of the straightaway, only to tie up and get passed, ending up in fifth, half a second from the win. It was a valuable lesson in sport psychology that the unexpected often happens.

In college, I learned the skill of visualization as I mentally rehearsed winning the conference championship at 800 meters my senior year, and just like Billy Mills, my visualization became reality in record time.

In graduate school at the University of Oregon, I was exposed to some of the top runners in the world that I competed and trained with. I was also fortunate to study with Olympic coaches. Those experiences have been invaluable in trying to understand how to improve performance both from a physical and mental aspect.

As a head collegiate and high school cross country and track and field coach, I began to understand the use of mental skills and drills to improve performance. I started using it with my college athletes, and in my third year, our team finished second in the national meet. I was just getting into implementing mental skills with the team and they bought in. Over the course of the season they continued to improve physically and mentally. I was sold on the value of mental skills and continued to implement it into practice and competition.

For over 30 years, I have taught at the college level and incorporated mental skills and drills into my teaching and development of young coaches. I get very excited when I see young, future coaches learn about mental skills. Many are similar in their experiences to what mine were. They were not previously exposed to a systematic mental skills program in their athletic experiences. Although most coaches and athletes agree that the mental side is very important, they do not engage in mental skills training. No, it is not that they are bad coaches, bad athletes, or bad people. It's just that they have not been exposed to a mental skills training program. All coaches would like mentally skilled athletes, but many don't have the knowledge to implement mental skills training. Athletes would like to be mentally skilled, but lack the knowledge of mental skills training. This book is for athletes and coaches that want to improve the mental game.

If you are an athlete, I am excited that you have chosen to improve your mental game and take your performance to the next level. If you are a coach, congratulations, you have the most influential occupation in the world. By learning about and implementing mental drills, you will be embarking upon a fruitful journey to improve mental skills and make a positive difference.

Mental Skills and Drills Athlete Workbook

Table of Contents

Preface 1

Chapter 1 .... Introduction to Mental Skills 5

Chapter 2 .... Finding Your Optimal Arousal Zone 15

Chapter 3 .... Goals 27

Chapter 4 .... Self-Talk 45

Chapter 5 .... Imagery 57

Chapter 6 .... Focus 67

Chapter 7 .... Mental Plans 79

Resources 89

About the Author 91

Chapter 1: Introduction to Mental Skills

Activity 1.1 asks you to determine how much of your sport is mental.

Activity 1.1: How much of athletics is mental?	
What percentage of your performance is mental?	_____
What percentage of your performance is physical?	_____
What percentage of your time do you spend training for the mental side?	_____
What percentage of your time do you spend training for the physical side?	_____
Many coaches and athletes believe a large percentage of their performance is mental but they don't train for the mental side. Could this be you?	
Think of how many times your performance suffered from a lack of confidence, focus or determination.	
Do you believe that mental training could improve your game? How could it improve it?	

Recall the details of one of your best performances ever in *Activity 1.2*.

Activity 1.2: Most Memorable Performance
Think of one of your best performances ever. It may be in a sport or it could be in something else, such as singing or giving a speech. Recall a time when you felt so good and everything came together perfectly. Recall it in as much detail as possible.
Where were you?
What were you doing?
How did you feel?
Why do you think you performed so well that day?

Activity 1.3 is a powerful demonstration of the mind/body connection.

Activity 1.3: Chevreul's Pendulum
Objective: To demonstrate the link between the body and the mind.
Directions:
Take a 6" piece of string and tie a small weight on it. It can be something like a key or a nail. Hold the string between your forefinger and thumb with the elbow supported on the table. The weight should be steadied to be motionless with your other hand. Hold the string so the key is above the intersection of two perpendicular lines below. Now remove your hand that is steadying the weight. Focus on the weight and see it going back and forth, sideways. See the weight move from one side of the paper to the other side, back and forth. Then, see the weight stop and move toward you and away from you. See it as it comes toward you and then away from you, toward you and away from you. You may be surprised to see the weight actually moving.
What happened? The mind is sending the message through the nerves for the muscle to contract. The muscles are contracting, but the contraction is so small that the string and weight have to be used to magnify the movement so that it can be visually seen. When you actually see the movements occur, it is a strong visual of the mind-body connection where just thinking about the movement causes muscle contraction.

Take *Activity 1.4: Mental Skill Training Quiz* to see what you know about mental skills training.

Activity 1.4: Mental Skills Training Quiz			
True or False			
1.	T	F	Athletes are born (innate) with strong mental skills.
2.	T	F	Mental skills training works immediately.
3.	T	F	Mental skills training is too time consuming.
4.	T	F	Mental skills training is only for psychological whackos.
5.	T	F	Mental skills training is only for elite athletes.
6.	T	F	Mental skills training is about performing miracles.
7.	T	F	Mental skills training guarantees a top performance at the right time.
8.	T	F	Mental skills training works by simply reading about it.
9.	T	F	Mental skills training is a substitute for physical conditioning and technique training.
10.	T	F	Mental skills training will not turn a loser into a winner.

Activity 1.5: Walk The Plank is designed to look at how a positive mindset and a negative mindset have two complete views in how to achieve a task.

Activity 1.5: Walk the Plank
Part 1:
Place a board (2 inch x 4 inch approximately 4-6 feet long) on the ground. Who would like to walk the plank? If you feel it is too dangerous to walk across the board, or are too nervous or scared of walking across the board as it lays on the ground, you are not required to walk across it. Go ahead and try walking the plank if you dare.
For thought:
Did you walk across the plank? How did you feel as you walked across the plank? Was it hard? Was it easy? Were you scared or nervous?
Part 2:
Imagine the same plank placed between two tall skyscrapers. The plank is placed out one window on the 100th floor to the adjoining skyscraper window on the 100th floor. The plank links the two skyscrapers. Underneath the plank, 100 floors down is the ground. Who would like to walk the plank now?
For thought:
Would you walk across the plank 100 stories high? What were your thoughts in making that decision?
Wrap up:
When the plank is on the ground, it is easy to walk over the plank. You feel confident of your abilities to walk the plank and your self-talk is confident. When the plank is placed 100 stories high, thoughts turn to the negative consequences. "What would happen if I fall? I would be flattened like a pancake when I hit the ground." Your mind has changed from thinking of the positive side of performance to the negative consequences of failing. What has changed in this scenario? The board has not changed. The mind has changed from a positive outlook to a negative outlook. This exercise illustrates the importance of positive thinking and self-confidence in achieving a successful performance.

Complete *Activity 1.6: Fight or Flight Response,* which provides another example of the mind-body connection.

Activity 1.6: Fight or Flight Response
Imagine that you and your buddy are hiking in the woods when you are suddenly confronted by a mean, hungry grizzly bear. What do you do? You don't have time to sit down and think about it. Actually, you only have to outrun your buddy! You have two choices: fight or flight. You can try to outrun the bear (or your buddy) or you can choose to fight the bear. When confronted by an emergency, the body has a natural response by the autonomic nervous system.
What does your body automatically do to prepare to run away from the bear or fight it?   1.   4.   2.   5.   3.   6.
Your body immediately responds physiologically. Your heart rate soars, your breathing goes up, your pupils dilate, and your hormones are called in to action! You may even pee your pants! This is an automatic response where what is perceived by your mind is immediately acted upon by the body. This mind-body connection is referred to as the "fight or flight" system.

Activity 1.7: Mugger or Jogger is an example of how the mind thinks and how the body reacts.

Activity 1.7: Mugger or Jogger
You are traveling and staying out of town. You go out for a walk, but end up getting lost. It becomes dark and you end up in bad part of town where the streetlights are out. It is a cold night and the wind is blowing. As you try to make your way back to where you are staying, you start to become uneasy with your unfamiliar surroundings. Suddenly, you hear footsteps behind you. Hearing the footsteps, you begin to pick up your pace, walking faster, but the footsteps are getting closer and closer. You walk even faster, but the footsteps continue to get closer. Someone is behind you and getting closer and closer to you. Who is behind you? How do you react?
If you said a mugger was behind you, the fight or flight physiological response was starting to kick in. Your heart would begin to race, you would sweat, the hormones would be activated and numerous other physiological responses would occur to prepare your body for action.
If you said it was a jogger behind you, would you have reacted differently? If you believed it was a jogger, you would have moved aside and encouraged the runner to have a good run. The way your mind interpreted the situation controlled how your body responded.

Activity 1.8: Think of Pizza is a fun activity that explores the power of the mind in concentrating.

Activity 1.8: Think of Pizza
Think of your favorite food. Think of how good it tastes. Think of how you would like to eat some of your favorite food right now. You can almost smell it and taste how good it is. It may be pizza, steak, seafood, candy, or ice cream. Now I want you to completely clear your mind of your favorite food. Do not think of your favorite food. Do not think of how good it tastes. Do not think of how you would like to eat some of your favorite food right now. Do not see yourself eating the favorite food. Whether it is pizza, steak, seafood, candy, or ice cream. Do not see yourself eating any of those favorite foods. What happened when you tried to not think of your favorite food? You still have that image of your favorite food in your mind; I know you do. Why? The brain does not know how to process and interpret the word "don't." The brain only understands what comes after don't, which in this case is, "think of your favorite food." You may tell yourself, "do not slow down" or "do not let my competitor pass me." You may say, "do not miss" or "do not foul." The brain does not know how to process and interpret the word "don't." The brain only understands what comes after don't, which in this case, is "think of your favorite food." Specifically, we only hear "slow down, miss, or foul" during competition. Has this happened to you? Have you told yourself not to do something in sport and then it happens? Can someone really stop thinking? Can you simply clear your mind? How do you relax? When someone tells you to concentrate, focus and pay attention, what are you supposed to focus on, concentrate on, and pay attention to?

One of the reasons you probably participate in your sport is because you like the kinesthetic feelings of physical movement. *Activity 1.9: Iron Arm* provides a physical example on the power of focusing on a mental thought.

Activity 1.9: Iron Arm
Part 1: Pair off with a partner (similar heights if possible) facing each other about an arm's length apart. Partner #1 sets an arm, palm facing up, on partner #2's shoulder. Partner #2 takes his/her hands and links them around partner #1's extended arm right above the elbow. Partner #1 is instructed to tighten his/her arm as much as possible so as not to let partner #2 bend it with his/her strength downward. Let each partner take a turn in both positions before moving on.
Part 2: Repeat the scenario, but this time, have the partners imagine a strong steel bar that extends through their arm making it tight and rigid. The steel bar gives them power and makes their arm unbendable. Once this image is created, have partner #2 push down on the arm. Let each partner take a turn in both positions.
For Thought:
In part 1, were you able to bend the arm of your partner? Was your partner able to bend your arm?
In part 2, were you able to bend the arm of your partner? Was your partner able to bend your arm?
What was the difference between part 1 and part 2? Why do you believe the difference occurred?
Wrap-up:
In most cases, when the image of the steel bar is created, the arm is much stronger than when the image is not created. Just imagining the arm is an iron bar made the arm stronger. The image from the brain was transmitted to the muscles to make them stronger. Imagine how this skill could be applied to athletics to help increase performance!

Read *Activity 1.10: Billy Mills: Believe-Believe-Believe*, a classic story of using positive self-talk and a belief in one's self to be successful in order to establish the relationship between mental training and athletic success.

Activity 1.10: Billy Mills: Believe-Believe-Believe **Excerpt from *Motivational Moments in Men's Track and Field*, Roho Publishing**
Billy Mills, a Native American (Oglala Lakota (Sioux)), was raised on the Pine Ridge Indian Reservation in South Dakota. He was orphaned at the age of 12. Mills took up  running while attending the Haskell Institute in Lawrence, Kansas. He attended the University of Kansas and earned All-American cross country honors three times. In 1960, he won the individual title in the Big Eight cross country championship. Billy helped lead the University of Kansas track team to the 1959 and 1960 outdoor national championships. After giving up running for a while, he returned to the sport to qualify for the 1964 Summer Olympics in Tokyo in the 10,000-meter run and the marathon. On October 14, 1964, 38 runners competed in the 10,000-meter final at the Tokyo Olympics. One of the starters was a virtually unknown in the track and field world. Billy Mills of the U.S. with a 10,000-meter best of 29 minutes 10.4 seconds was not expected to be a contender for the medals. However, Mills, who had faced discrimination and difficult times his entire life, believed in himself. As he trained for the Olympic Games, he visualized over and over, running the race. In his mind he saw himself running with the leaders and winning! He repeated over and over to himself the affirmation: Believe-Believe-Believe. The favorite, world-record holder Ron Clarke (Australia), led most of the way with a quick pace. With one lap remaining, Clarke had dropped all his main rivals, but he still had two athletes with him, Mills and Mohamed Gammoudi of Tunisia, both relatively unknown, and both running much faster than they ever had before. The three were hindered by lapped runners on the last lap who made no effort to let them through on the inside. In the back straight, Clarke bumped Mills, pushing him to the outside lanes and causing him to drop back about four meters. At this point, Mills focused on his affirmations: Believe-Believe-Believe, as Gammoudi and Clarke sprinted for the finish. Gammoudi had shaken off Clarke and seemed to have the race won with 50 meters to go before Mills came storming past both of them to win the gold medal. Billy's winning time of 28 minutes 24.4 seconds was a personal record by 50 seconds and a new Olympic record. The race has been called the greatest upset in Olympic history and Mill's victory remains the only Olympic 10,000-meter win in U.S. Olympic history.
Questions For Thought: Why was Billy Mills' race so surprising? How did Billy Mills prepare himself mentally to run in the Olympic Games? How can you apply the story of Billy Mills to help improve your mental skills?

Billy Mills was a very motivated athlete. Think of an athlete that you are familiar with. Maybe they are on your team or a role model or mentor to you.

Complete *Activity 1.11: The Motivated Athlete,* to explore the characteristics of a motivated athlete who used mental training for success.

Activity 1.11: The Motivated Athlete
Think of the most motivated athlete you have ever seen. Who was it? Why do you think they were motivated? Were they motivated by fear? Were they motivated by extrinsic rewards? Were they optimistic? What sense of purpose did they have?

Interviewing successful athletes who use mental training can be inspiring. *Activity 1.12* provides example questions that could be used.

Activity 1.12: Questions for Interview/Guest Speakers
What role did mental skills play in your success?
Did you engage in mental skills training? How did you do it?
How much time did you devote to mental training?
What do you owe your success to?

Every day, either online or in the sport section of most newspapers, there are excellent examples of the mental side of sport. Use *Activity 1.13* to find motivational stories of the successful use of mental training.

Activity 1.13: Media Examples
Search the media on the Internet, or newspapers and magazines for examples of mental skills used by elite athletes. Are the examples positive or negative?

Before you start your program, let's find out where you are at right now on your mental game. Complete *Activity 1.14: How's Your Mental Game?*

Activity 1.14: How's Your Mental Game?					
For each question, circle the appropriate number on the scale. Never / Sometimes / Always					
1. I talk positively to myself.	1	2	3	4	5
2. A bad performance never gets me down.	1	2	3	4	5
3. I keep working even when I am physically tired	1	2	3	4	5
4. I am excited about going to practice every day.	1	2	3	4	5
5. I handle anxiety and pressure well.	1	2	3	4	5
6. I imagine myself performing flawlessly.	1	2	3	4	5
7. I block out distractions so I can concentrate.	1	2	3	4	5
8. I handle frustration well in practice.	1	2	3	4	5
9. How often do you set goals to help you achieve?	1	2	3	4	5
10. I work with my goals on a daily basis.	1	2	3	4	5
Total Score _____					
If you scored 10-20, you are in the beginning stages of learning how to become stronger mentally. Absorb all you can.					
If you scored 21-30, you are making some headway, but still have much to learn. Jump in headfirst.					
If you scored 31-40, you are building a solid mental fitness program. Keep up the good work. Adding mental tools to your mental toolbox will take you to the next level.					
If you scored 41-50, you have a strong mental fitness profile. Congratulations! By adding more mental tools to your toolbox, think about how good your performances can be!					

Chapter 2: Finding Your Optimal Arousal Zone

Complete *Activity 2.1: Where on The Arousal Continuum Am I?* to better understand different levels of arousal.

Activity 2.1: Where on the Arousal Continuum Am I?	
Place an X on the continuum line where you believe your arousal level would be for each situation.	
	Sleep Excitement --- Low Moderate High
Reading this	---
Watching TV	---
Moments before a big competition	---
During a hard workout	---
Taking a test you are prepared for	---
Taking a test you are not prepared for	---

Use *Activity 2.2* as you chart where you are on the arousal curve during your best and worst performances.

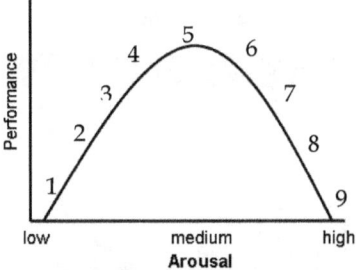

Activity 2.2: Psych Number									
Think of your three best performances. Remember how you felt before and during those performances. Rate how you felt on each variable on a scale of 1-9.									
Best Performances	Low								High
Muscle Tension	1	2	3	4	5	6	7	8	9
Heart Rate	1	2	3	4	5	6	7	8	9
Breathing	1	2	3	4	5	6	7	8	9
Doubts/Worry	1	2	3	4	5	6	7	8	9
Negative Thinking	1	2	3	4	5	6	7	8	9
Think of your three worst performances. Remember how you felt before and during those performances. Rate how you felt on each variable on a scale of 1-9.									
Muscle Tension	1	2	3	4	5	6	7	8	9
Heart Rate	1	2	3	4	5	6	7	8	9
Breathing	1	2	3	4	5	6	7	8	9
Doubts/Worry	1	2	3	4	5	6	7	8	9
Negative Thinking	1	2	3	4	5	6	7	8	9
Was there a difference between your best and worst performances in your ratings? What numbers do you think you performed best at?									

Activity 2.3 asks you to assess your arousal levels during practice or competition.

Activity 2.3: Finding Your Proper Arousal Level
Arousal Monitoring Scale

During practice or competition assign yourself an overall score. Over time you will discover what your number is when you are at your best and at your worst. You will find over time what your optimal arousal level will feel like.

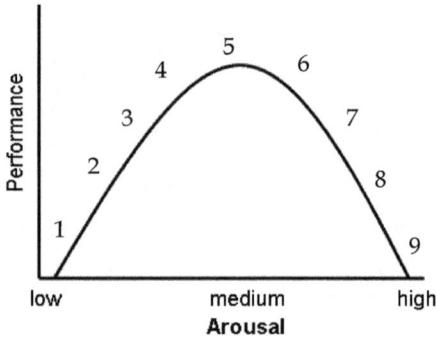

Complete *Activity 2.4: Hot or Cold* to help find your proper arousal level using the thermometer method.

Activity 2.4: Hot or Cold

Using the following thermometer to rate what degree temperature you are operating for the following?

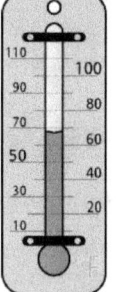

Best Performances
Temperature Range

_____

Worst Performances
Temperature Range

_____

Is there fluctuation in your performance?

Compare your better and poorer performances. What were the temperature levels?

Were there changes in preparation activities? What preparation activities led to your optimal temperature?

Complete *Activity 2.5* to determine "what it takes to be great."

Activity 2.5: What does it take to be great?			
Develop a list of physical and mental characteristics that you feel are essential for consistent, high level performance. Think of the ideal athlete in your event. What are the mental and physical characteristics that make them ideal? Some of the characteristics you might consider would be: confident, determined, focused, positive, coachable, calm. After you have listed the characteristics, rate yourself on each physical and mental characteristic on a scale of 1-10 with 10 being high. Place your number to the right of the each characteristic.			
Physical Characteristics	Your Rating	Mental Characteristics	Your Rating

In *Activity 2.6: Bubble Blowing*, we will start with a simple and fun technique to illustrate how breathing can relax you.

Activity 2.6: Bubble Blowing
1. Start with a bottle of bubbles.
2. Take a deep inhalation and fill your lungs of air.
3. Now as you exhale, slowly blow bubbles.
4. See how big of bubble you can blow.
5. As you get good at blowing bubbles, and more importantly relaxing as you exhale, you can try the following.
a. Think about a worry that is bothering you and picture that you are blowing the worry into the bubble as you blow a bubble
b. Picture the worry inside the bubble.
c. Watch it float away and pop, carrying the worry far, far from you.
d. Know that the worry has popped and is outside of you now, unable to bother you any more.
6. Keep blowing bubbles until you feel more calm and relaxed.
For Thought:
Do you feel more relaxed? Do you feel less worried? Were you able to picture your worries floating away in the bubbles?

In *Activity 2.7: Sequential Relaxation*, the focus should be on experiencing deep levels of total relaxation.

Activity 2.7: Sequential Relaxation
Assume a comfortable position and when ready, allow your eyes to close. Turn your attention to the exhalation phase of our breathing cycle… and r-e-l-a-x as you exhale… exhale and r-e-l-a-x…permit yourself to let go… and r-e-l-a-x more and more with each exhalation.
Now focus on your right foot and ankle and as you exhale notice the tension flow out of that foot and ankle… note the foot and ankle becoming slightly heavy and more and more relaxed… As you notice this, allow the foot and ankle to sink down and become totally supported by the floor. As you exhale, notice the sinking down of your foot into the supporting environment.
Now focus your attention on the left foot and ankle… and allow it to let go and r-e-l-a-x with your exhalations allow that foot and ankle to become slightly heavy… and more and more relaxed with each exhalation.
Now move your focus to your right lower leg (the calf region). As you focus on this area, allow the muscles to relax… to let go as you exhale… simply allow the tensions to flow out of the lower leg as you e-x-h-a-l-e and r-e-l-a-x.
Move your attention to the left lower leg and with each exhalation, feel the muscles of the left lower leg sinking down… and becoming slightly heavy.
Move your attention to the thighs and feel that body part r-e-l-a-x as you exhale and relax. Feel and experience a letting go with each exhalation.
Let the relaxation flow into the buttocks and hips… As you exhale, allow the muscles to

> relax and feel the buttocks sinking down into the supporting environment.
>
> Let the relaxation flow into the trunk area as you e-x-h-a-l-e and r-e-l-a-x. Feel the trunk sinking down and becoming slightly heavy as you continue to e-x-h-a-l-e and r-e-l-a-x.
>
> Move the attention to your arms and hands. Feel the relaxation flowing into the arm and hand. Feel it sinking down as you feel the gentle pull of gravity exert itself on the arms and hands.
>
> Allow this relaxation to flow into the entire body with each exhalation. Feel sense and experience a comfortable heaviness... a general slowing down of the body... Allow the body to establish its own pace... and r-e-l-a-x as you exhale.

Activity 2.8 is a fun activity that will illustrate progressive muscle relaxation. These activities are very familiar to the popular foam roller exercises. You will need a foam sponge ball or a tennis ball for this activity.

Activity 2.8: Tennis Ball Relaxation

1. Grip the ball in your hand. Squeeze the ball and hold for five seconds. As you release the tension in your grip feel the muscles relax.
2. Place a ball underneath the arch of your foot. Keep your heel on the floor and let your body weight sink in. You may want to stand next to a wall or chair for stability.
   a. Take deep breaths for 30 seconds to 1 minute.
   b. Slowly roll your foot from side to side so the ball crosses your arch. Repeat for 1 to 2 minutes
   c. Roll the ball along the length of your foot from heal to toe for 1 to 2 minutes.
   d. Repeat on the other foot.
3. Knee
   a. Sit on the floor or in a chair and place the ball behind your bent knee.
   b. Attempt to contract your muscles against the ball, temporarily "squashing" the ball for a count of 10, then relax your muscles for a count of 10. Do this 8 to 10 times.
   c. Repeat on the other knee.
4. IT Band
   a. While lying on your side on the floor, place 2 balls on the outside of your thigh. Keep the balls nestled into the side of your thigh and slowly bend and straighten your knee 20 times.
   b. Move your thigh from side to side so that the balls cross the side of your thigh. Repeat for 2 minutes.
   c. Repeat on the other side.
5. Lower Back
   a. Place 2 balls vertically between your buttocks and your ribs and lie down on top of them. Breathe deeply while shifting your pelvis from side to side so the balls cross your entire lower back.
   b. Move the ball more slowly in the areas where you feel stiffer, and lighten your pressure when you're near the spine so that you're not pinching the balls into your bones as you cross from right to left or left to right.
   c. Breathe deeply as you roll for up to 5 minutes.
6. Upper Back
   a. Lie down and place two balls side by side on either side of your upper back. (You can place them in a tote, stocking, or sock, if you'd like.) Interlace your hands behind your head and lift your head off the floor, bringing your chin toward your chest. Lift your bottom off the floor and take 3 deep breaths into

> your ribs.
> b. Keeping your breaths big and steady, roll the balls like a rolling pin up and down your upper back for 3 to 4 minutes.
> c. These are just a few of the tennis ball activities you can do to contract, stretch and relax. I encourage you to try the tennis ball on other parts of your body to help relax.

Activities 2.9 to *2.13* are relaxation exercises. Try them out and see which ones work best for you.

Activity 2.9: Progressive Muscle Relaxation

1. Begin by finding a comfortable position sitting, standing, or lying down. You can change positions any time during the progressive muscle relaxation exercises to make yourself more comfortable as needed.

2. The first progressive muscle relaxation exercise is breathing. Breathe in forcefully and deeply, and hold this breath. Hold it… hold it… and now release. Let all the air go out slowly, and release all the tension. Take another deep breath in. Hold it… and then exhale slowly, allowing the tension to leave your body with the air.

3. Now breathe even more slowly and gently… breathe in…hold…out… Breathe in…hold…out…Continue to breathe slowly and gently. Allow your breathing to relax you. The next progressive muscle relaxation exercise focuses on relaxing the muscles of your body. Start with the large muscles of your legs. Tighten all the muscles of your legs. Tense the muscles further. Hold onto this tension. Feel how tight and tensed the muscles in your legs are right now. Squeeze the muscles harder, tighter… Continue to hold this tension. Feel the muscles wanting to give up this tension. Hold it for a few moments more…. and now relax. Let all the tension go. Feel the muscles in your legs going limp, loose, and relaxed. Notice how relaxed the muscles feel now. Feel the difference between tension and relaxation. Enjoy the pleasant feeling of relaxation in your legs.

4. Now focus on the muscles in your arms. Tighten your shoulders, upper arms, lower arms, and hands. Squeeze your hands into tight fists. Tense the muscles in your arms and hands as tightly as you can. Squeeze harder… harder… hold the tension in your arms, shoulders, and hands. Feel the tension in these muscles. Hold it for a few moments more…. and now release. Let the muscles of your shoulders, arms, and hands relax and go limp. Feel the relaxation as your shoulders lower into a comfortable position and your hands relax at your sides. Allow the muscles in your arms to relax completely.
Focus again on your breathing. Slow, even, regular breaths. Breathe in relaxation…. and breathe out tension… in relaxation…and out tension… Continue to breathe slowly and rhythmically. Now focus on the muscles of your buttocks. Tighten these muscles as much as you can. Hold this tension… and then release. Relax your muscles.

5. Tighten the muscles of your back now. Feel your back tightening, pulling your shoulders back and tensing the muscles along your spine. Arch your back slightly as you tighten these muscles. Hold… and relax. Let all the tension go. Feel your back comfortably relaxing into a good and healthy posture.

6. Turn your attention now to the muscles of your chest and stomach. Tighten and tense these muscles. Tighten them further…hold this tension… and release. Relax the muscles of your trunk.

7. Finally, tighten the muscles of your face. Scrunch your eyes shut tightly, wrinkle your nose, and tighten your cheeks and chin. Hold this tension in your face… and relax. Release all the tension. Feel how relaxed your face is.

8. Notice all of the muscles in your body... notice how relaxed your muscles fee l. Allow any last bits of tension to drain away. Enjoy the relaxation you are experiencing. Notice your calm breathing... your relaxed muscles... Enjoy the relaxation for a few moments...When you are ready to return to your usual level of alertness and awareness, slowly begin to re-awaken your body. Wiggle your toes and fingers. Swing your arms gently. Shrug your shoulders. Stretch if you like.

Activity 2.10: Complete Diaphragmic Breathing

Sit or lie down in a comfortable position. Close your eyes and concentrate on taking complete breaths. Inhale through the nose, causing the diaphragm to move down. Gently place one hand on your stomach, just above your belly button, but below your rig cage. Now focus on making your hand rise and fall as you inhale and exhale. You will feel the breathing as your diaphragm expands and your abdomen is pushed out. Next, as the middle portion of your lungs fill, your rib cage expands. Finally, your upper lungs fill and you feel your chest and should raise slightly. After the complete inhalation, pause and then complete a slow exhalation through the mouth. Complete 4 breaths that require you to breathe in a manner that allows you to use your full lung capacity. If you are doing this exercise properly, your hand should move up and down with each breath. Now take two - three minutes and focus exclusively on making each breath deep and complete. As you do so, be aware of how your body becomes more and more relaxed and your mind becomes calm and focused.

Activity 2.12: Short Version: Breathing - Relaxation

Assume a comfortable position, sitting or lying down and when ready, allow your eyes to close. Concentrate on your natural breathing rhythm. Notice how it feels as you inhale and exhale. Turn your attention to the exhalation phase of our breathing cycle. And r-e-l-a-x as you exhale... exhale and r-e-l-a-x...permit yourself to let go... and r-e-l-a-x more and more with each exhalation. As you inhale, feel the energy coming into your body and as you exhale feel the tension flowing out of your body, inhale-energy in, exhale-tension out. Continue to focus on your exhalations as you exhale and r-e-l-a-x. Maintain your focus on your breathing for a few minutes. If you get distracted, notice the source of the distraction and then gently bring your focus back to your breathing. You will become relaxed and experience a state of peacefulness. When ready, stretch, and open your eyes.

Activity 2.13: Autogenic Breathing

Sit or lie down in a comfortable position. Close your eyes, take a couple of deep breaths, and focus your attention on the muscles throughout your body. As you discover tension, let it drain out of your body. Throughout this exercise, you will be asked to focus on the bodily sensations of warmth and heaviness. These feelings occur when the body is relaxed and comfortable. Begin by focusing your attention on your breathing ... (pause for 2 or 3 seconds with each). With each breath, your head becomes heavier... heavier... warmer... warmer...

Now shift your focus to your arms and hands. With each breath, your arms and hands become heavier... heavier...heavier...warmer... and warmer... Now concentrate on your buttock, legs and feet. With each breath your buttocks, legs, and feet become heavier... heaver.... heavier...warmer.... warmer... warmer.

Now as you relax, notice your torso becoming heavier...heavier... heavier...warmer... and warmer... Be aware of your entire body as it becomes heavier... heavier... heavier... ...warmer... warmer... warmer... Feel how heavy your entire body has become and notice the warmth of your experience as you enjoy relaxation and peacefulness.

Activities 2.14 to *2.20* use rapid relaxation and cue words that will allow you to achieve optimal arousal.

Activity 2.14: Relaxing Quick Breathing

1. Inhale deeply and feel the air fill your lungs as your chest rises.
2. Exhale and blow the air out of your lungs, feeling relaxed.
3. As you exhale repeat a cue word such as "relax" to yourself.
4. Repeat two to three times.

Activity 2.15: Whoosh Power Breathing

1. Blow out one noisy "whoosh" exhaling through your mouth, puffing out your cheeks. Blow as much air as possible out of your lungs to prepare for a deep inhalation to flood fresh air into your lungs.
2. Take a deep breath through your nose. Make it a power inhalation from your abdomen. Make sure you do not raise your shoulder or puff on your chest. Imagine the tension being pulled from your lungs by a vacuum cleaner.
3. Blow out another loud "whoosh," hearing the air as it is exhaled. Imagine the tension leaving your body as you exhale.
4. For just a few quick breaths, focus on inhaling energy in, and "whooshing" tension out.

Activity 2.16: Standing Abdominal Breathing

In a standing position, place your hands on your sides, with your thumbs pointing backwards and positioned in the hollow above each hip. Your fingers extend forward, resting on your abdomen and stretching just below your navel.

Take a deep breath and feel your abdomen swell beneath your fingers and thumbs. Make sure your shoulders do not rise and your chest does not puff out.

Exhale slowly and evenly until you feel your abdomen fall under your fingers.

Take one or two full exhalations that push the air from the bottom of your lungs.

Activity 2.17: Quick Scan and Release

1. Scan your body for any tension and then consciously release tension found in any muscles.
2. Focus on the muscles you will be using for your performance.
3. You may want to add some specific stretches to this technique so you can release the tension in the tight muscles (e.g. rolling the head in a slow circle for the neck muscles to relax).

Activity 2.18: Chill Pill

Identify three situations in which you could use a rapid relaxation response. Practice this situation now and how you would handle it. When the situation arises later in the day use the rapid relaxation technique to lower your arousal level.

	Relaxation Technique Used
Situation 1	
Situation 2	
Situation 3	

Activity 2.19: Relaxation Words

1. Pick a word that relaxes you.
2. Close your eyes and focus on taking relaxing breaths.
3. With each exhalation, say your cue word.
4. Do this for one minute and then stop repeating your cue word.
5. Focus on how your body feels in this relaxed state for a few minutes.
6. Start repeating your cue word again on each exhalation for one minute.

Activity 2.20: Cued Relaxation

Perform a total relaxation technique that works for you.

Pair a cue word with the feeling of being highly relaxed.

Repeat your cue word after each third relaxation breath for a total of 10-15 repetitions. The cue word chosen should have a strong relaxing influence (such as relax, calm or cool).

Use cued relaxation to promote rapid relaxation within 5 seconds by taking 5 relaxation breaths and repeating your cue word. When you master this technique, you can quickly achieve your proper arousal level within seconds.

Activities 2.21 to *2.27* are energization techniques to raise arousal level into the optimal zone.

Activity 2.21: Energizing Imagery

Close your eyes and begin to focus on your breathing. With each inhalation think of energy "coming in" and with each exhalation think of "tension out." With each inhalation, feel your muscles becoming more and more powerful. See your body as a powerful machine. Visualize performing your sport and performing it with high energy and power.

Activity 2.22: Music

Many athletes already use music to relax and it can also be used as an energization technique. Up-tempo music provides an energizing effect. The music tends to enhance energy levels at a sub-conscious level. The rhythm of the music helps to trigger energization as the athlete plays a song mentally in their mind. An athlete might mentally replay a tune that helps them feel powerful and explosive while getting ready to perform. An athlete might use a fast paced song or feel the rhythm of a song.

Activity 2.23: Energy at the Top of the Mountain

Close your eyes and take several deep breaths. Feel your diaphragm expand, your chest expand, hold the breath briefly and then exhale. With each breath, you relax more and more completely.

Picture yourself at the bottom of a mountain. You slowly begin to climb up the mountain, smooth and effortlessly. With each step, you become more and more energized, more rejuvenated with more vitality. As you continue to climb and go higher, you continue to build strength, power, and energy. With each step, you feel the adrenaline and more full of energy than the last step you took.

When you reach the top of the mountain, you stand on top of the world. You feel close to the bright sun, absorbing the energy. As you absorb the sun, feel the mountain tremble. As you feel the tremble, feel the energy transfer from the ground to your body, filling you full of power and energy from the feet to the top of your head. Feel the energy pulsate through your body, bringing a confident attitude. Feel the energy invigorate your legs, strength and power radiating through your feet. The waves of pulsating energy fill your lower body with strength and power, full of stamina and endurance. Your muscles tingle with energy. Feel your heart pumping oxygen to every muscle in your body.

Feel the energy spread through your upper body, pushing strength and power through your chest, shoulder, back and arms. Feel the power growing with each breath. Every muscle fiber in your body is poised for a peak performance, just waiting for a challenge or goal to accomplish. You are totally positive, energized, and ready to meet the challenge.

Count 15 breaths, each time repeating your energization cue word after each set of three psych-up breaths. As you say your cue word, focus your mind on the feelings of energization throughout your body.

Activity 2.24: Psych-Up Breathing

Psych-up breathing is quick, shallow breathing to quickly transport oxygen to the working muscles. The quicker breathing rhythm requires athletes to breathe shallowly with the lungs instead of with the diaphragm. The emphasis is on the inhalation phase where you should feel energy flowing in with each breath. Psych-up breathing is very effective in elevating arousal.

Once you have practiced psych-up breathing, it is time to link a cue word to it. Practice linking energization and cue words in *Activity 2.25* and *2.26*.

Activity 2.25: Energizing Words
1. Pick a word that energizes you.
2. Close your eyes and focus on taking energizing breathes.
3. With each exhalation, say your cue word.
4. Do this for one minute and then stop repeating your cue word.
5. Focus on how your body feels in this relaxed state for a few minutes.
6. Start repeating your cue word again on each exhalation for one minute.

Activity 2.26: Energization and Cue Words
1. Perform a total energization technique that works for you.
2. Second, pair a cue word with the feeling of being highly energized.
3. Repeat your cue word after each third psych up breath for a total of 10-15 repetitions. The cue word chosen should have a strong energizing effect (such as power, strong, or energy).
4. Use cued energization to promote rapid energization with 5 seconds by taking 5 quick psych-up breaths and repeating the cue word. When you master this technique, you can quickly achieve your proper arousal level within seconds.

Activity 2.27: Activate the Body
Another simple way to energize is to physically activate the heart rate and body by clapping your hands, jumping in place, or running in place.
What other quick activations could you do to energize and achieve the proper arousal zone?
1. _____
2. _____
3. _____

How effective you have been at achieving your proper arousal level in the past. There is no score at the end, but view this as a self-discovery activity that will provide you with information to guide you in achieving your proper arousal level for future practice.

Use *Activity 2.28* to determine how effective you have been in achieving your "optimal level of arousal."

Activity 2.28: Self-Evaluation of Optimal Level of Arousal

Consider what you have done in the past to increase or decrease your own level of arousal to be able to perform at your best. Rate your effectiveness of getting into your proper arousal zone. Use a scale of 1-10. 1=not effective, 10=very effective

How effective have you been in decreasing your level of arousal?

1. Downplaying the importance of the event — 1 2 3 4 5 6 7 8 9 10
2. Slowing down the warm-up — 1 2 3 4 5 6 7 8 9 10
3. Changing your focus — 1 2 3 4 5 6 7 8 9 10
4. Using total relaxation techniques — 1 2 3 4 5 6 7 8 9 10
5. Using rapid relaxation techniques — 1 2 3 4 5 6 7 8 9 10
6. Using cue words — 1 2 3 4 5 6 7 8 9 10
7. Stretching and exercising — 1 2 3 4 5 6 7 8 9 10
8. Breathing — 1 2 3 4 5 6 7 8 9 10
9. Music or videos — 1 2 3 4 5 6 7 8 9 10
10. Imagery — 1 2 3 4 5 6 7 8 9 10

How effective have you been in increasing your arousal level?

1. Reminding yourself of your goals — 1 2 3 4 5 6 7 8 9 10
2. Short bursts of high intensity effort — 1 2 3 4 5 6 7 8 9 10
3. Using cue words — 1 2 3 4 5 6 7 8 9 10
4. Breathing and self-talk — 1 2 3 4 5 6 7 8 9 10
5. Energizing imagery — 1 2 3 4 5 6 7 8 9 10
6. Energizing verbal cues — 1 2 3 4 5 6 7 8 9 10
7. Energy from the environment — 1 2 3 4 5 6 7 8 9 10
8. Using total energization techniques — 1 2 3 4 5 6 7 8 9 10
9. Using rapid energization techniques — 1 2 3 4 5 6 7 8 9 10
10. Breathing — 1 2 3 4 5 6 7 8 9 10

Chapter 3: Goals

An important part of the initial goal setting process is understanding why you participate in your sport. Complete *Activity 3.1: Why I Participate* to review why you're in your sport.

Activity 3.1: Why I Participate
Think back to the first time you participated in your sport. Why did you decide to start participating in your sport?
When you first started, what did you enjoy about your sport? Think about your participation now in your sport. Why do you still participate in your sport?
What do you enjoy most about your sport now?

Use *Activity 3.2: Why Set Goals* to think about the important process of goal setting.

Activity 3.2: Why Set Goals
List three reasons why you believe it is important to set goals.   1.   2.   3.
Wrap-Up:
You may have thought about the following reasons: Goals will give you purpose and direction. Well-designed goals will help motivate, promote self-confidence, and increase performance. Goals also enhance concentration and create a positive attitude.

Overwhelming evidence exists that goal setting is one of the most effective strategies available to enhance performance. The key to goal setting success lies in how you set your goals. Complete *Activity 3.3: My Goals* to start learning how to properly set goals.

Activity 3.3: My Goals
List four goals you have for the upcoming season. We will come back and address your goals a bit later in this chapter.   1._____   2._____   3._____   4._____

Fill-In 3.1: Types of Goals

Types	Characteristics	Example
1.		
2.		
3.		
4.		

Activity 3.4: What Type of Goals Do I Set

Now, let's go back and look at what you wrote down for Activity 3.3. Identify the type of goal you wrote, as either outcome, performance, process or effort.

Goal 1: _____ Goal 2: _____ Goal 3: _____ Goal 4: _____

How would you revise your goals now that you know the types of goals and benefits of each goal?

Table 3.1: Goal Continuum

Effort Goals--------Process Goals--------Performance Goals---------Outcome Goals

How do you feel competent regardless of winning or losing? Re-define success as achieving effort and process goals. Placing your focus on effort and process goals is a path that you have control over.

Table 3.2 gives examples of the different types of goals.

Table 3.2: Goal Type Examples

Effort	Process	Performance	Outcome
Run hard to first base every time	Obtaining the proper arousal zone	Increase leg strength by weight training	Beat the throw to first
Use a positive mental attitude at all times	Use trigger words of smooth, explode and kick	Bat .400	Win the state title
Box out on the rebound	Visualize perfect technique prior to each jump.	Progressively increase jump heights throughout the season	Go undefeated

Activity 3.5: Writing Smart Goals

Column one lists a negative goal. In column two change the negative goal to a positive goal. Use the examples as a guideline.

Being Positive	
Negative Goal	**Positive Goal**
I don't want to get cut	I will make the team
I don't want to slow down	I will finish strong
I won't make any stupid mistakes	I will use my cue words to focus and be confident
1.	1.
2.	2.
3.	3.

Specific	
Non-Specific Goal	**Specific**
I will get more sleep	I will get 8 hours of sleep per night by going to bed at 10:00 p.m.
1.	1.
2.	2.
3.	3.

Measurable	
Non-measurable	**Measurable**
Eat less candy	I will eat 4 servings of fruits and vegetables every day.
1.	1.
2.	2.
3.	3.

Aggressive but Achievable	
Non-Aggressive/Achievable	**Aggressive/Achievable**
I will show up at practice every day.	I will come to practice with focus and ready to get better every day.
1.	1.
2.	2.
3.	3.

Relevant	
Non-Relevant	**Relevant**
I will be the Olympic champion.	I will get better every day by working on my mental skills every day.
1.	1.
2.	2.
3.	3.

Non-Time	Time
I will shoot 100 free throws.	I will shoot 100 free throws every day.
1.	1.
2.	2.
3.	3.

Outcome goals tell you where you want to be, which can help motivate. But, on a daily basis, they do not tell you what you need to do. By changing outcome goals to process goals, you will be in control of your goal program. Complete *Activity 3.6* to *Change Outcome Goals to Process Goals*.

Activity 3.6: Change Outcome Goals to Process Goals

1. Start With an Outcome Goal

Choose an upcoming competition, and pick a challenging but not impossible outcome goal (win, place, get a certain score or time, etc.). Write that goal down in detail here:

My outcome goal:
_____
_____

2. Moving From Outcome to Process Goals

How can you maximize your chances to achieve this goal? Write down three things (i.e. improve technique, mental training, weight training, plenty of sleep) you can do in order to reach your goals. Be specific.

    1. I will: _____

    2. I will: _____

    3. I will: _____

3. Practicing the Process and Effort Goals in Training

What can you do in practice between now and your competition to help you towards your process goals? These could include effort goals. For example, if your competition task goal is to hold a specific pace, you might focus on that pace in practice.

1. In training, I will
_____

2. In training, I will
_____

3. In training, I will
_____

Activity 3.7 is a goal sheet form that focuses on short-term goals (30-60 days or less) and long-term goals, which would be season-long goals. *Activity 3.8* is the same concept as *Activity 3.7*, but includes a place for affirmations that are associated with each goal.

Activity 3.7: Example Goal Sheet With Affirmations

Goal #1

Run a 4:50 1600 or faster
Goal #1 Affirmation:
I work hard toward my goals.

Steps to attain this goal:

1. Increase endurance by running 2 mornings a week

2. Workout every weekend

3. Use visualization for 5 minutes three times a week

4. Be mentally strong in practice by visualizing a good workout before practice

Affirmation for each step:

1. Morning runs make me tough.
2. I am committed to being a better runner.
2. Mental training makes me great.
4. I am prepared for a great practice effort.

Goal #2

Run the 3200 meters under 10:00 minutes
Goal #2 Affirmation:
I am focused on reaching my goal.

Steps to attain this goal:

1. Use affirmations during challenging periods in practice

2. Set goals for my races and practices

3. Commit to reaching my practice and race goals

4. Visualize running a sub-10 3200 3x a week

Affirmation for each step:
1. I use my cue words to make me stronger.
2. I have a plan for success.
3. I am committed to my plan for success.
4. I am a great distance runner.

Goal #3-Lifestyle Goal

Adapt a lifestyle conducive to being a great runner.
Goal #3 Affirmation:
My lifestyle makes me a better athlete.

Steps to attain this goal:

1. Practice mental training everyday

2. Eat carbohydrates within 2 hours of each workout

3. Limit fast food to no more than three times per week

4. Get at least 8 hours of sleep every night-
   be in bed by 10:00 p.m.

Affirmation for each step:

1. Proper sleep gives me the energy for great running.
2. I recover quickly.
3. I eat nutritiously to improve performance.
4. Mental training makes me tough.

Summary for the week:

Strengths:
_____
_____
_____

To work on:
_____
_____
_____

Comments:
_____
_____
_____

Week of _____ to _____

Name _____ Signature: _____ Date: _____

Partner Name _____ Signature: _____ Date: _____

Activity 3.8: Weekly Goal Sheet With Affirmations

Goal #1

Goal #1 Affirmation:

Steps to attain this goal:

1. _____
2. _____
3. _____
4. _____

Affirmation for each step:
1. _____
2. _____
3. _____
4. _____

Goal #2

Goal #2 Affirmation:

Steps to attain this goal:

1. _____
2. _____
3. _____
4. _____

Affirmation for each step:
1. _____
2. _____
3. _____
4. _____

Goal #3-Lifestyle Goal

Goal #3 Affirmation: _____
_____

Steps to attain this goal:

1. _____ ☐☐☐☐☐☐☐

2. _____ ☐☐☐☐☐☐☐

3. _____ ☐☐☐☐☐☐☐

4. _____ ☐☐☐☐☐☐☐

Affirmation for each step:
1. _____
2. _____
3. _____
4. _____

Summary for the week:

Strengths:
_____
_____
_____
_____

To work on:
_____
_____
_____
_____

Comments:
_____
_____
_____
_____

Week of _____ **to** _____

Name _____ **Signature:** _____ **Date:** _____

Partner Name _____ **Signature:** _____ **Date:** _____

Activity 3.9: Weekly Goal Sheet without Affirmations

Goal #1

Goal #1 Affirmation:

Steps to attain this goal:

1. _____
2. _____
3. _____
4. _____

Goal #2

Goal #2 Affirmation:

Steps to attain this goal:

1. _____
2. _____
3. _____
4. _____

Goal #3

Goal #3 Affirmation: _____
_____

Steps to attain this goal:

1. _____ ☐☐☐☐☐☐☐
2. _____ ☐☐☐☐☐☐☐
3. _____ ☐☐☐☐☐☐☐
4. _____ ☐☐☐☐☐☐☐

Summary for the week:

Strengths:
_____
_____
_____
_____

To work on:
_____
_____
_____
_____

Comments:
_____
_____
_____
_____

Week of _____ to _____

Name _____ Signature: _____ Date: _____

Partner Name _____ Signature: _____ Date: _____

Activity 3.10: Short and Long Range Goals Without Affirmations

Short Range Goals (daily or 30 days or less)

I. _____

Three steps to attain this goal:

    a. _____

    b. _____

    c. _____

II. _____

Three steps to attain this goal:

    a. _____

    b. _____

    c. _____

III. _____

Three steps to attain this goal:

    a. _____

    b. _____

    c. _____

I am willing to make sacrifices and make the commitment to be a great runner!

_____ _____ _____
Print your Name   Signature   Date

Long Range (Season) Goals

I. _____
_____

Three steps to attain this goal:

    a. _____

    b. _____

    c. _____

II. _____
_____

Three steps to attain this goal:

    a. _____

    b. _____

    c. _____

III. _____
_____

Three steps to attain this goal:

    a. _____

    b. _____

    c. _____

I am willing to make sacrifices and make the commitment to be a great runner!

Print your Name	Signature	Date

Activity 3.11: Short and Long Range Goals With Affirmations

Short Range Goals

I. _____

Three steps to attain this goal:
    a. _____

    *Affirmation for this goal: _____

    b. _____

    *Affirmation for this goal: _____

    c. _____

    *Affirmation for this goal: _____

II. _____

Three steps to attain this goal:
    a. _____

    *Affirmation for this goal: _____

    b. _____

    *Affirmation for this goal: _____

    c. _____

    *Affirmation for this goal: _____

III. _____

Three steps to attain this goal:
    a. _____

    *Affirmation for this goal: _____

    b. _____

    *Affirmation for this goal: _____

    c. _____

    *Affirmation for this goal: _____

_____   _____   _____
Print your Name   Signature   Date

Long Range Goals With Affirmations

I. _____

Three steps to attain this goal:

    a. _____

    *Affirmation for this goal: _____

    b. _____

    *Affirmation for this goal: _____

    c. _____

    *Affirmation for this goal: _____

II. _____

Three steps to attain this goal:

    a. _____

    *Affirmation for this goal: _____

    b. _____

    *Affirmation for this goal: _____

    c. _____

    *Affirmation for this goal: _____

III. _____

Three steps to attain this goal:

    a. _____

    *Affirmation for this goal: _____

    b. _____

    *Affirmation for this goal: _____

    c. _____

    *Affirmation for this goal: _____

_____   _____   _____
Print your Name   Signature   Date

Table 3.3 provides recommendations and reminders on how you can focus on your goals throughout the day.

Table 3.3: Working With My Goals

When do I read my goals?
    1.   I read my goals 9 times a day.
           a.   I read my goals three times when I first get out of bed.
           b.   I read my goals three times during lunchtime or before practice.
           c.   I read my goals three times before I go to bed.
    2.   I read my goals out loud if possible.
 	
Where will I place my goals at home?
    Bathroom
    Mirror
    Desk
    Bedroom
Where will I place my goals when I take them with me?
    In cell phone
    On note card
    In diary
 	
        If I read my goals, and believe my goals, I will achieve my goals.

Complete *Activity 3.12: Draw Your Individual Goal* and *Activity 3.13: Draw Your Team Goal*. I recommend sharing your team goal picture with your teammates in a show and tell session.

Activity 3.12: Draw Your Individual Goal

What does your goal look like? See your individual goal in as much detail as possible and then draw it. Draw yourself achieving your goal. You may want to use color to bring it to life!

Activity 3.13: Draw Your Team Goal

What does your team goal look like? See your team goal in as much detail as possible and then draw it. Draw your team achieving your team goal. You may want to use color to bring it to life!

Activity 3.14: Progress Evaluation

Give yourself a rating on a scale of 1-10 (with 10 being high) of how you are doing.

	Rating
1. My performance in practice overall	
2. My performance in warm-up	
3. My performance in using proper goals on a daily basis	
4. My performance in drills	
5. My effort on a daily basis	
6. My attitude on a daily basis	
7. My performance in weight training	
8. My attention and contribution to team meetings	
9. My encouragement of teammates	
10. My positive attitude	
11. My lifestyle outside of practice	
12. Use of affirmations to perform better	
13. Effectively using mental training during practice	
14. Using mental training outside of practice	
15. Proper sleep	
16. Proper nutrition	
17. Good hydration practices (drinking water)	
18. Ability to push myself	
19. Contribution to team	
20. Progress toward my goal	
21. Number of times a week doing mental training	

Chapter 4: Self-Talk

Activity 4.1 illustrates the "power of being positive."

Activity 4.1: The Power of Being Positive
Find a partner and face each other. Person 1 closes their eyes and extends their arms out to the side like a cross. Person 2 stands in front of Person 1 and grasps the wrist of Person 1. Person 2 instructs Person 1 to think of something that makes them sad and feel negative. When Person 2 gets this in his head, he nods his head. Person 2 then puts Person 1's arms down, while Person 1 attempts to keep his arms up.
After the arms are pushed down, the two people exchange places and repeat the exercise. After both have completed with a sad thought, they both do the exercise with a positive, happy and energizing thought.
For thought:
Compare the two different exercises.
Was there a difference? What was the difference? Why did the difference occur?
Wrap-up:
Normally, people are much stronger when thinking positive thoughts. The exercise demonstrates the thoughts that affect the energy level of the body and overall performance.

Use *Activity 4.2* to record what you say to yourself.

Activity 4.2: My Self-Talk Log		
Select three positive and three negative situations from a practice or a competition. A positive situation is an event in which you execute correctly, show improvement, demonstrate team unity or have fun. Briefly, describe each situation and highlight the positive nature. Then record the specific positive thoughts you recalled. For example in learning a new skill it might be, "I got it!" "I want to try it again!" Repeat the process for up to three negative situations in practice or competition in which there was poor performance. Describe each negative situation and identify the specific negative thoughts you had during the experience.		
My Self-Talk Log Day _____		
Positive Situations	**Positive Thoughts**	**Effect on practice or competition**
1.		
2.		
3.		

Negative Situations	Negative Thoughts	Effect on practice or competition
1.		
2.		
3.		

Wrap-up:
Is your self-talk harmful or helpful?

Fill-in 4.1: 5 P's of Affirmations
P
P
P
P
P

If you are having trouble assessing positive and negative situations, then record a PMA (Positive Mental Attitude) score for each day in *Activity 4.3*.

Activity 4.3: My PMA Scores							
Record a PMA (Positive Mental Attitude) score for each day. Rate your PMA from 1 to 10, with 1 being the most negative day of your life, 5 an average day and a 10 the most positive day of your life. The PMA score should represent the quality of the day.							
	Monday	Tuesday	Wednesday	Thursday	Friday	Saturday	Sunday
Week 1							
Week 2							
What did you learn from the exercise?							

Use *Activity 4.4: Effective Use of Affirmations* to develop your understanding of the effective use of guidelines.

Activity 4.4: Effective Use of Affirmations		
In column 1, an example affirmation is given. In column 2, there is information on why the affirmation needs improving and in column 3, there is a re-write for an improved affirmation. Read the examples provided in 1-5 and then create your own affirmation and fill in columns 2 and 3 for numbers 6-10.		
Affirmation Examples	**Why it needs improving**	**Improving the affirmation**
1. I will not slow down	Stated in negative terms	I focus on maintaining correct pace!
2. I've tried in the past	Turn into present tense	I give a great effort every day!
3. Shoot better	Not personal	I am a great shooter!
4. I jump	Needs more power	I explode off the floor!
5. I will get around to it	Get to the point	My training makes me powerful!
6.		
7.		
8.		
9.		
10.		

Now that you have a better understanding of the guidelines to develop affirmations, complete *Activity 4.5: My Affirmations*.

Activity 4.5: My Affirmations		
Fill in the following chart, listing five affirmations that might apply to your sport. In column 1, list your affirmation. Review your affirmation. How could you improve it? List how you could possibly improve your affirmation in column 2. In column 3, rewrite your affirmation to make it better.		
Original Affirmation	**How to Improve?**	**Improved Affirmation**

You are well on your way to developing good affirmations and improved self-talk. Now let's take a look at the difference between general and specific affirmations. *Activity 4.6* gives three examples of general affirmations and three examples of specific affirmations.

In the blank space provided after the examples, list three general affirmations and three specific affirmations. If you become stumped on what affirmations to use you might want to take a look at *Table 4.1*, which lists several general affirmations.

Activity 4.6: General and Specific Affirmations	
General Affirmations Examples	**Specific Affirmations**
1. I am strong	1. I spike the volleyball with power.
2. I run with power	2. I explode out of my stance.
3. I am relaxed and focused	3. I attack the goal.
Your General Affirmations	**Your Specific Affirmations**
1.	1.
2.	2.
3.	3.

Table 4.1 lists several general affirmations.

Table 4.1: General Affirmation Examples
I am **strong**.
I am **relaxed**.
I am **confident** and **ready**.
I am in **control** and **focused**.
I am physically tough and mentally **tough**.
I train harder and **smarter** than my opponents.
My **determination** and **drive** makes me a winner.
I accept the **challenge** and the body responds.
My enthusiastic **attitude** makes me great.
I have the **courage** to perform.
My weight training, diet, sleep, and mental training all help me to **perform** better.
When fatigue sets in, I am mentally **tough.**
My form **is fluid, smooth, controlled** and **relaxed.**
I **seize** the moment. I make my own **opportunities.**
I am always **positive.**
I am willing to do the **extra** things to be great.
I am **fit.**
I am a **competitor.**
My **training** and **attitude** make me great.
I enjoy training and reaching my **goals**.

Activity 4.7 asks you to come up with your own general and specific cue words.

Activity 4.7: Cue Word List	
General Cue Words	
Focus	Ok
Calm	Do it
Relax	Control
Tight	Confident
Add five more general cue words	
1. _____	
2. _____	
3. _____	
4. _____	
5. _____	

Specific cue word examples	
Go	Push
Fast	Explode
Run	Catch
Swing	Cast
Up	Steady
Land	Straight
Twist	Leap
Power	Explode
Pull	Stick
Add five more specific cue words	
1. _____	
2. _____	
3. _____	
4. _____	
5. _____	

Use *Activity 4.8: Building Confidence* to reflect on your past success.

Activity 4.8: Building Confidence
Make a list of your successes in your sport and other areas. Reflect on this success and the effect that the success has had on your present level of confidence. Use this list to remind you of your talent and effort during times you are unsure of yourself.
1.
2.
3.
4.
5.

Now you are starting to understand the importance of being positive and how we can use self-talk to develop a positive mindset. The challenge is figuring out how to maintain that positive attitude and how to keep it when confronted with negative thoughts.

Mentally strong athletes reframe situations in order to perform their best. By using their mental skills, they create a positive mindset that promotes success rather than allowing the situation to dictate how they think and react. Use *Activity 4.9* to reframe situations into a positive challenge.

Activity 4.9: Re-Frame your Thoughts	
Take the self-defeating thoughts in column 1 that interfere with personal excellence and re-frame those thoughts in column 2. Examine the first five thoughts and use those as examples to provide five thoughts that may self-defeat you and how you can reframe those thoughts.	
Self-Defeating Thoughts	**Re-Framed Thought**
You idiot.	Everyone makes mistakes.
I have no talent.	I can get better if I practice. Good athletes work hard to be successful.
The other athletes are better than me.	You cannot control other athletes, focus on your own abilities.
I'll take it easy today and go hard next time.	Going hard today makes it easier next time.
This hurts, is it worth it?	It hurts, but the rewards are worth it.
1.	
2.	
3.	
4.	
5.	

Activity 4.10 is similar to the Re-Framing Thoughts Activity in that it asks you to change limiting factors into strengths. In order to make those changes, add affirmations to reinforce the project.

Activity 4.10: Stinking Thinking
Limiting Factors
Write down three factors that limit you from becoming a great athlete. Example factors might be no endurance, not willing to work hard, lack of mental toughness.
Changing Limiting Factors to Strengths
For each factor listed above, write down what you could do to change the limiting factor into a strength.
Get Rid of Limiting Factors
Take a pen or maker and cross out what you have written previously under limiting factors. Mark it out, so you cannot read it. You have taken the negative factors that limit you and eliminated them from your life. Now, let's turn our attention to the positive strengths.
Affirmations
For each of the factors listed under Changing Limiting Factors To Strengths, write an affirmation that will help you to make a positive change!
Wrap-up:
You can write your limiting factors on a slip of paper. Once you have written your changed factors to strengths, you can make a ceremony out of getting rid of the stinking thinking thoughts. Wad the paper up and slam it into a trashcan, or if possible and you can safely do so, burn it!

Activity 4.5 looks at identifying the negative and positive thoughts that you have in practice, before a competition, and during a competition. Make sure you examine the differences carefully. If you do not have many positive thoughts, work on changing your negative thoughts into positive ones.

Activity 4.11: Changing Negative Thoughts to Positive Thoughts	
Thoughts I have in practice…	
Negative Thoughts	**Positive Thoughts**
1	1
2	2
3	3
What can I do to change these negative thoughts into positive thoughts?	
Thoughts I have before or during a competition…	
Negative Thoughts	**Positive Thoughts**
1	1
2	2
3	3
Read your comments and form a picture of what you say to yourself. Read the positive things and relate them to your performance. How did they help you stay focused and to try harder? Did they make you feel good about your performance? Read the negative thoughts. Were there more negative thoughts than positive? When did the negative thoughts occur? What happened to your focus and your performance when you listened to them? How did they distract, limit, or defeat you?	

Activity 4.12: Self-Talk Exercise lists several specific points in a competition. List the cue words that you might use to help stay positive during the competition.

Activity 4.12: Self-Talk Exercise	
In the table below, column 1 lists specific points in a competition. In column 2, provide positive cue words (such as prepared, ready, strong, and control) you would like to say to yourself before and during the competition. See if you can come up with three cue words for each point. Take this sheet and commit your cue words to memory. When you visualize your performance try to incorporate these cue words to make the whole visualization seem more real.	
Specific Points	**Cue Words**
1 hour before the competition	
5 minutes before the competition	
Start	
First ¼ of the competition	
Middle of the competition	
The finish of the competition	

In *Activity 4.13*, you will develop a confidence card, an important tool that allows you to re-focus on your performance.

Activity 4.13: Confidence Card
Use a 3" x 5" or 4" x 6" card. Write down on the card three affirmations that give you confidence in your abilities. These should be words that you have visualized and used in practice to succeed. These are you confidence words that you believe in. When you repeat them, the feelings of confidence will flow into your body. If you wish, you can add pictures or color to your card. You might highlight cue words. You may also want to include on your card any other comments that will bring you confidence. When you feel anxiety and nervousness before a competition or even a practice, take a couple of deep breaths to relax and then take out your card to look at. Take three deep breaths and repeat an affirmation after each one.

Example of Confidence Card:
 I am PREPARED I am STRONG My POSITIVE attitude makes me a GREAT athlete! I have worked hard in workouts. I have had some great practices. I will use the same confidence that I use in hard workouts to enable me to succeed today. *I will do my best.* RELAX! BELIEVE! BE A COMPETITOR! SUCCEED!

A power picture combines the power of a visual image with the positive cue words that are meaningful to you. *Activity 4.14* should be a fun and meaningful activity. Use a picture where you are looking good so every time you see it you feel the power!

Activity 4.14: Power Picture

Directions:

Find a good picture of when you are competing. Make sure the picture shows you in good form and looking strong. Put the picture on a page (preferably cardstock paper). Place your cue words around the picture.

When you look at the picture with your cue words surrounding it, you should feel powerful, positive thoughts.

Your self-worth is not related to your athletic performance. Use *Activity 4.15* to realize how many things you are good at.

Activity 4.15: I'm Good At

Objective: To realize you are good at many things.

Directions: List 10 things that you are good at. These can be athletic on non-athletic related. After you get 10, go for 20!

1.	11.
2.	12.
3.	13.
4.	14.
5.	15.
6.	16.
7.	17.
8.	18.
9.	19.
10.	20.

For Thought:

Was it difficult to come up with 20 things you are good at?

Why or why not?

Did you find yourself writing down athletic things you were good at when you started the list?

Wrap-up:

Often athletes associate their self-worth with how they are performing athletically. When their athletic performance is poor, their self-worth becomes poor. Unfortunately, that can lead to mental health problems. Although it is not the scope of this book to deal with mental problems, realizing that you are good at many things, including things that are not athletic related, will help you to realize you are a well-rounded person. Athletics is only one of the things that you are good at.

It is important to talk to yourself in a positive manner. *Activity 4.16* is a sample script that can be used for athletes. I encourage you to use the self-talk script as guide and develop your own personal, meaningful script.

Activity 4.16: Positive Self-Talk Script for an Athlete
I like to learn. I like to learn about things I will use the rest of my life, for my family, and for my career. Going to school with a positive learning attitude gives me the opportunity to learn the skills I can use for my lifetime. With all the learning experiences I am receiving, I am confident I will be successful. Although every day is not perfect, I have people to help me. These friends and family care about me and help me to succeed. I enjoy spending time with my friends, but I also enjoy my time alone. This time allows me to relax and think positive. I like who I am and I don't feel that I have to impress others. I like my sport because the challenge makes me feel good. I know the challenges of my sport will make me better. They will make me stronger and help me become a better athlete. I like to work hard. It makes me successful and I enjoy stepping up and meeting the challenges. I like the satisfaction of knowing that I have given it my all. I enjoy being a role model in practice and leading by example. I am confident that my hard work and effort also helps my teammates become better. The harder I work, the better I get and the better my teammates get. Although I am busy, I have time to get everything done because I effectively manage my time. I like being busy and accomplishing many things because it makes me a better person.

Chapter 5: Imagery

Activity 5.11 illustrates the power of imagery.

Activity 5.1: Eating a Lemon
In your mind, see a lemon. Notice the bright yellow color of the lemon; see how smooth and shiny it is. Pick up the lemon and feel it in your hands...slide your fingers over the smooth skin of the lemon...feel the texture of the lemon. Lift the lemon to your face and breathe in that lemon smell. Now slice the lemon open, see the bright yellow flesh exposed and see the juice run out. Smell the lemony citrus aroma filing the room. You cut a slice and put it into your mouth...bite down on it...and feel the juice run over your tongue and your mouth fills with sour lemon juice.
For Thought: Were you able to clearly visualize the experience of a lemon in your mind?
Wrap-up: Recalling eating the lemon recalls your distinctive reaction to your past experiences with a lemon and your body responds with a conditioned reflex. The Eating a Lemon visualization exercise demonstrates that words have a profound physical effect on the body.

Fill-in 5.1: Types of Imagery	
Types of Imagery	**Definition**
Mental Recall	
Mental Rehearsal	

Activity 5.2 evaluates your ability to use your senses in imagery.

Activity 5.2: Sensory Checklist		
This is an exercise designed to help you integrate your senses into your imagery. Rate your ability to create each of the following images in your mind on a scale of 1-10.		
Scale: 0 = No image	5 = Some image	10 = Very clear image
The place you are currently in		____
Tasting a juicy lemon		____
The clothes you will wear in practice		____
The last place you competed		____
The feeling at the end of an exhausting workout		____
Practicing or competing on a very cold, windy day		____
The applause of spectators		____
The anticipation and anxiety before your event		____
Tasting your favorite food		____
Performing a drill related to your event		____

Memories can leave a powerful image. Use *Activity 5.3* to help connect the relationship between imagery and memories.

Activity 5.3: Imagery Association		
In column one there is an experience that you have associated memories with. For each experience, list some associated memories in column two, and in column three list why it is a strong memory.		
	Associated Memories	Why a strong memory?
Least Favorite Foods		
Mom		
Favorite Song		

Use *Activity 5.4* to imagine yourself improving a past performance.

Activity 5.4: You are in Control
1. Imagine working on a specific skill that has given you trouble in the past.
2. Notice what you are doing wrong.
3. Now see and feel yourself performing that skill perfectly.
4. Think about a troublesome competitive situation in the past. See yourself being positive and performing in the clutch.

Use imagery logs to help track how you will use imagery. When you learn new skills, you can monitor your progress by having a written record. Determine how you will use imagery and keep tabs on what you do, how much you do, and when you do it. You can look back and see your progress.

Activity 5.5: Imagery Log				
Date	Time	Describe Imagery	Practice Time	Success
3/25	1:30 pm	Shot 20 free throws	5 min	A little trouble seeing makes

Most people can see images, but the rest of the senses can be more difficult to experience. Use *Activity 5.6: Sensory Imagery* to help improve using all your senses. An example using basketball is provided

Activity 5.6: Sensory Imagery
Directions: Close your eyes and imagine in as much detail as possible.
Vividness: Imagine a basketball. Notice the orange color. Notice how round it is.
Auditory: What sounds do you hear while you are playing basketball?
Tactile: Imagine holding the ball. What does it feel like? Notice its shape and roundness. Feel how light the ball feels as you rotate the ball in your hand. Note how hard it feels as you squeeze it.
Kinesthetic: Imagine shooting the ball during warm-ups. Feel what your body is doing during the shooting. Feel the muscles in your leg moving as you move into the proper position, feel the muscles in your shoulder and arms as you bring the ball forward to shoot. Note the tempo and rhythm of the shot. Do a couple of shadow shots with or without holding the ball, but do not actually shoot.
Smell: Smell the ball, the court, and the facility. Smell the sweat after a hard practice.
Taste: Taste the salt from the sweat on your lips. Imagine taking a drink of water.
Emotion: Experience the confidence you feel when you step into the floor. Experience the satisfaction of making a shot. Experience the excitement of being on a successful team.
Vividness Evaluation: What were the strongest images and sensations? What senses do you need to improve?
Follow-up: Certain senses may produce clearer attention than others. Use this exercise to provide direction for extra attention and practices.

The ability to visualize includes the ability to dream of accomplishing goals. Use *Activity 5.7: Sports Headline* to write your own story.

Activity 5.7: Sports Headline
Imagine the local newspaper reporter is at your next sporting event. You have a great performance and as soon as you are done competing, the reporter rushes up to you to interview you about your outstanding performance. Create the sports headline and write the story of what will run on the front page of the sports section. Headline:_____ Story:_____ _____ _____ _____
Variations: (1) Type the report up, (2) add a picture to the story, (3) add an action picture if possible

Making vivid images that you control are extremely important as a performance enhancement tool. You control the image and see what you want to see happen. Use *Activity 5.8: Control the Outcome* and *Activity 5.9: Imaging Skills* to gain control of your vision.

Activity 5.8: Control the Outcome

1. Approach a competition area where you have competed and have vivid memories. Imagine how you want to be feeling:

What I want to be saying to myself:

2. Imagine yourself at varying times before competition.
How I want to be feeling:

What I want to be saying to myself:

3. Imagine yourself during competition.
How I want to be feeling:

What I want to be saying to myself:

4. Imagine yourself after competition.
How I want to be feeling:

What I want to be saying to myself:

Controlling the imagery at times may become difficult. You may see images of what typically happens rather than what you want to happen. As it is counterproductive to image scenes you cannot control and which will lead to undesirable outcomes, stop the imagery. Rewind or repeat the imagery and start over.

Activity 5.9: Imaging Skills

As you refine your ability to image with all of your senses, it is important to use imagery to see yourself performing your sport. Work through the progression at your own pace. If you can't image yourself performing sports skills right now, keep working on your practice situation and movement imagery until they are vivid and controllable.

1. Imagine you are at the venue where you usually practice.
Use your imaging skills to see your practice environment. Look around the area and imagine in as much detail as possible:
    Feel the court or field under your feet
    Imagine yourself in your practice gear
    Imagine yourself holding and using the ball or implement
What are some other things you can incorporate into this image form where you practice?
    a.
    b.

2. Movement Imagery
Feel yourself:
    Walk around the area
    Run around the area
    Do some warm-up stretches
    Take warm-up throws, shots, or runs
See other skill movements in your events

Follow-up:
What was easy to image?
What was hard to image?
Did you have a hard time using one sense or another?
Could you see some things and not others?

Homework for Later: Practice the images that were harder to create.

Creating imagery and associating with the actual experience is a vital link that can be accomplished with practice. Use *Activity 5.10: Act Like* to help complete that link.

Activity 5.10: Act Like
Creating a specific image (object, animal, or person) can aid in your creation of images. In the following space, pick a skill you are working on in practice and choose an image to pair with that skill. **Examples:** **Skill:** Running relaxed and fast **Image:** Gazelle **Affirmation:** I run like a gazelle. **Skill:** Throwing **Image:** Dynamite **Affirmation:** I explode like dynamite.
Skill: **Image:** **Affirmation:** How will this image help?
Skill: **Image:** **Affirmation:** How will this image help?
Skill: **Image:** **Affirmation:** How will this image help?

Instant replay gives us the ability to see an event over and over. *Activity 5.11: Rewind It* asks you to see an image over and over to get a clearer picture of it.

Activity 5.11: Rewind It
Imagine yourself performing your event for 30 seconds. It can be helpful when you're having difficulty controlling your imagery to slow it down, in which you see and feel yourself performing in slow motion, frame by frame. As you gain imagery control in slow motion, you can progressively increase the speed of your imagery until you are able to perform at real speed. When you see a mistake or think negative thoughts, rewind your image and play that part over. Watch yourself performing on an actual video then immediately close your eyes and reproduce the video images. As the visual image of how you perform becomes clearer, put away the video for a while and repeat the accurate visual images of your performances. If the image starts to fade, return to the video until you're able to see yourself perform consistently. This exercise will help you ingrain an accurate image of how you perform.

In Chapter 2, the focus was on achieving your proper arousal by using relaxation techniques. Imagery can be a valuable tool for achieving relaxation or energization to achieve the proper arousal level. Try *Activity 5.12: Using Imagery for Relaxation* to achieve a relaxed state of mind.

Activity 5.12: Using Imagery for Relaxation
You can effectively calm yourself down by using your imagination to mentally take yourself to a calm, safe place. Sit quietly, close your eyes, and imagine yourself going to a totally relaxing place like a favorite beach, mountainside, woods, or vacation spot. Experience yourself comfortably enjoying this place in as much detail as possible, seeing, hearing, and feeling everything that you would as if you were actually there. Allow yourself to stay in this calming place for 5 – 10 minutes at a time until you feel calm, relaxed and in control.
Regular "visits" to this mental "relaxation room" will make it available to you under pressure, right before that big competition and right before your event. However, if you never consistently practice this exercise at home when you're completely relaxed, then you'll find that it won't be "open" and available for you when you need it the most.

Activity 5.13: Mentally Recalling a Great Performance is an example of a mental recall. It involves recalling an event when you were at your best. Since you have already achieved what you are about to visualize, you do not need to be in a relaxed state.

Activity 5.13: Mentally Recalling a Great Performance
Think of one of your best performances ever. It may be in your sport or it could be in something else, such as singing or giving a speech. Recall a time when you felt so good and everything came together perfectly. Recall it in as much detail as possible. Performance #1 Where were you? _____ What were you doing? _____ How did you feel? _____ Why do you think you performed so well that day? _____ Performance #2 Where were you? _____ What were you doing? _____ How did you feel? _____ Why do you think you performed so well that day? _____

Activity 5.14 is an example of a mental rehearsal. It involves imaging an event before it happens. I encourage you to do a brief relaxation exercise to achieve a relaxed state before beginning.

Activity 5.14: Goal Achievement Visualization
Begin to think of a time in our life when you were "right on" and performed perfectly. See yourself at that time… notice what you look like, what you are wearing, who is with you, what sounds are around you. Feel the environment and the energy. Begin to see yourself doing whatever it was you did when you knew you were right on… when everything worked perfectly… when you were in complete control and at your peak… Feel that feeling as you watch yourself and connect with all the feelings you experienced as you achieved at your highest level… perfectly…competently… exactly the way you wanted to. What did it feel like… sound like… look like…Let it all come back to you… let it in… know it again… the joy… the power… the pride and confidence … the completeness… the rush of knowing you were perfection… let it become part of you…part of your spirit…part of your being. Fully connect with it. Now give yourself a word or short phrase that brings all these feelings, pictures and

sounds into focus, a word or phrase that completely connects you with that time and those feelings when you knew you were perfect and right on...say the word or words to yourself several times... slowly allow yourself to experience your sense of power ... feel it in your whole body.

Think of your goal... what you want to achieve now... the importance it has for you... Remember how it felt to write it down and see it on paper. Begin to see yourself preparing to accomplish this goal. Where are you? What do you look like? Are there other people there to assist you? How will they assist you? Begin to go for your goal... feel yourself starting... moving toward your goal... toward your personal fulfillment. Give yourself permission to have it just the way you want it to be.... See it perfectly as you move closer and closer to your goal... feel that excitement and rush that comes with doing something well...flawlessly and with control...Connect with your excellence as you reach and attain this important goal... let yourself have it...feel it...see it...know it completely... Say your special word or phrase... know those feelings... that power ... see your peak performance... exactly the way you want it to be.

I encourage you to make your own personalized rehearsal script specific to your sport. *Activity 5.15: Personalized Rehearsal* gives ideas on how you can write your own script.

Activity 5.15: Personalized Rehearsal

Objective: To write a personalized guided mental script. In your own words, write a mental rehearsal of an upcoming performance. This visualization will let you see, hear, and feel yourself performing your sport.

Directions:
Write a personalized guided visualization script. Be as specific as possible. Include as many senses you can. Write it down as full and complete as you can. Remember to use positive statements and include your affirmations. Use the worksheet to formulate your ideas. Then, write out your guided visualization in an essay format. After writing the visualization, I would encourage you to record the script. Find a quiet time to play some relaxation music and then play your recorded script. As you talk to yourself, see the visualization coming to life!

Worksheet for your guided visualization

Preparation Period
    See yourself in the preparation phase leading up to the event
    What have you done well?
    Think of some of your best workouts
    Focusing on your goal and the outcome you wish to achieve
Day of the Event
    See yourself getting up in the morning with confidence
    What will you have to eat?
    See yourself dressing for the competition, putting on your clothing
Arriving at the Site
    See yourself arriving at the site
    See the competition
    See the environment, weather, temperature
    Focus on your goal and the outcome you wish to achieve

The Warm-up
- See yourself doing your general warm-up
- See yourself stretching, drills
- See yourself doing your final preparations
- See yourself putting on your competition shoes

First part
- See yourself at the beginning of your event
- Hear the start of the event
- See yourself performing well, just the way you want to

The Middle
- See yourself right where you want to be
- See yourself in perfect position
- Feel yourself under control and on top of your game
- Feel yourself competing

The Finish
- Although fatigued, you feel confident
- Think of all the workouts that have prepared you for this
- Focus on your form and affirmations
- See yourself finishing strong

Post Event
- Feel the satisfaction of a job well done
- See teammates, coaches, family and friends congratulating you
- As you cool down, you feel good about your performance

As you go through your rehearsal, keep these guidelines in mind. Take your time to enjoy, to learn, and to experience each movement and moment.

1. As you arrive at the event, mentally rehearse going through your normal preparatory routine and the few minutes before you perform.
2. Go into vivid detail about the event and your experience of it, including sounds, colors, smells, the crowd, the weather, the positive feelings in your body and your mental state.
3. Imagine yourself being totally relaxed, confident, powerful and in complete control of your body and mind.
4. Include your affirmation and key words that will help you during your real performance.
5. Go through your whole event thinking of each significant point. Feel yourself moving smoothly and perform with strength and endurance.
6. Write your rehearsal in script form, reread it and edit it. Then dictate it to yourself or have someone else dictate to your recorder.
7. Listen to the recorded rehearsal for flaws and make changes to the script.
8. Dictate a progressive relaxation section that you feel will relax you effectively before the visualization.
9. Listen to the finished audio frequently.

Activity 5.16: General Mental Rehearsal Script

See yourself at the area you will be competing... wearing your competition clothes... your mind is on your performance. Notice everything that you can picture and feel in your mind about the competition area. You notice your competition... but you remain calm, confident, and relaxed. You feel really good. You are looking forward to competing and you have a feeling of being well-prepared. You are feeling good both mentally and physical. Your hard work and sacrifices are paying off! See yourself doing your normal warm-up routines... see whatever else you do to get ready for competition. As you are doing your warm-up, hear yourself say your positive affirmations. Hear the positive talk that keeps you focused and positive on the task at hand.

After you have completed the warm-up... see yourself taking off your sweats... doing your final stretches... and whatever you need for final preparation. Feel yourself before the event... feel the racing of the heart and pumping of the adrenaline throughout the body. Feel yourself perform your favorite rapid relaxation technique with your cue words. You are confident... you know you are ready to compete.

Now, see yourself at the event as it is about to start. Feel the familiar pounding of your heart and the familiar dry mouth feeling... the excitement and anticipation that flows through your body... the energy that will soon be turned into a great performance. As you start your event, it feels good... you are under control and establish your game. Feel the power that was stored up and now is unleashed... you are moving effortlessly... feel the strong powerful drive of the legs... feel your shoulders and arms relaxed. You are moving smoothly and fluidly. See yourself at the top of you game... doing whatever sport you do. See and feel it all coming together perfectly... just the way you want it.

You are saying your affirmations to yourself... you feel some slight fatigue... but your body is rising to the challenge. Say your cue words associated with your skills and feel your body step up to the challenge and respond. Visualize key points in your event... seeing yourself performing just the way you want to... perfectly... competently... you are in the flow and it feels great.

You have set yourself up in perfect position for crunch time. This is the point at which your hard training and confidence in yourself are paying off. You focus on your form... quick feet... staying relaxed. You are a competitor and you compete all the way. See and feel yourself performing the final part of your event. Visualize exactly what you expect to be happening... as you dig down for that last burst of power... you maintain your form to finish strong!

What a feeling of satisfaction. You performed exactly as you planned... you were strong, confident, and powerful... all your training is paying off... you are strong both mentally and physically. Hear the coach come up to you and tell you how well you performed! The feelings you are experiencing right now, you wouldn't trade for anything. See your teammates and friends congratulate you... listen to the excitement in their voices... see the smile on your face... hear what they are saying to you.

This is a special moment that no one can take from you. You have done your best and you are satisfied... take time to thank your heart, your legs, and your lungs.

Begin to let go of this image and this feeling... slowly re-enter your present space... feel your body... move your toes... move your fingers... begin to notice your breathing... inhale... exhale... inhale... exhale. You feel relaxed and filled with a new quiet energy.

Chapter 6: Focus

Let's start off by doing *Activity 6.1: Catching Markers* to illustrate the important of knowing what to focus on.

Activity 6.1: Catching Markers
You will need 10 different colored magic markers to try the following "focus test." Your task is to throw all 10 markers up at the same time above your head and try to catch as many as possible. It is important that when you attempt to catch them, you only use your hands and your hands must be away from your body (no trapping the markers against your body). Now, throw all 10 up at the same time.
How many did you catch?
If you do this correctly without cheating, then like most people, you probably only caught 1 or 2 at most.
Does that mean your ability to focus is very low? Absolutely not! This is an impossible task because there are too many things to focus on all at once. The fact of the matter is: YOU CAN ONLY CONCENTRATE ON ONE THING WELL AT A TIME. While you can focus on many things at once, when it comes down to peak performance, you can only focus on one thing well at a time. You better make sure that the one thing you are focusing on is WHAT'S IMPORTANT!
Now, pick one special marker in your group of 10 to focus on. For example, let's say the red one. Take that marker, stick it in the middle of the other 9 and throw all 10 up once again at the same time. Remember, you are focusing on catching only the one red marker.
What happened?
If you didn't catch the red marker the first time, try it again. If you have relatively decent hand-eye coordination, then you'll be able to catch that red marker.

Some examples of attentional dimension are provided in *Table 6.1*. To understand how dimensional attention works, read *Mental Skills and Drills for Athletes*.

	Table 6.1: Attentional Dimensions Example		
	Broad	**Broad**	
Internal	You decide to pass when the pace slows	Realize situation	External
Internal	Check arousal level and use cue words	See the ball flying through the air	External
	Narrow	**Narrow**	

Activities 6.2 and *6.3* will help you increase your concentration and focus.

Activity 6.2: Concentration Exercise

Practice these exercises on a daily basis for a couple of weeks. Do at least 10 minutes of the previous exercise everyday as your sport psychology homework. How else will you get better if you don't practice?

1. Listen to outside sounds (Broad External): Lie down with eyes closed and just concentrate on the sounds in the environment. (3 minutes)
2. Broad Internal: Monitor sounds of your body: Lie on your back with your eyes closed and fingers in your ears. Focus on all the sounds of the body- growling of stomach, breathing, heartbeat, etc. (2 minutes)
3. Narrow Internal: Flowing thoughts. Lie down and pay particular attention to thoughts that your mind brings to the surface. Perform this with a passive attitude. Recognize the thoughts and allow them to come into and leave the mind at your own pace. (2 minutes)
4. Narrow External: Study an object. Take a small object that can be manipulated in the hand (such as a coin, paper clip, ring) and focus internally on this object. If the mind begins to wander, refocus on the object. Each time you perform this exercise, change the object. (5 minutes)
5. Pick a problem (Narrow Internal): Pick an issue and ask your mind to give you as many solutions as it can. As the mind presents each solution, place it into a bubble and allow it to slowly flow away. Quietly wait on the next solution to appear. (5 minutes)
6. Narrow Internal: Listen to your own heartbeat. Close eyes while in a comfortable position and listen to your heartbeat. Attempt to hear nothing but your own heart beating. (3 minutes)

Activity 6.3: Learn to Focus

1. Take some time and focus on your breathing. See how long you can be aware of your inhalations and exhalations and the movement of your chest without allowing your mind to wander.
2. Pay attention to sounds around you. Notice any voices or noises in your environment. Focus on the noise you hear.
3. Focus on how your body feels. Feel your arms, head, neck, shoulders, stomach, and legs. Notice the feeling of the chair you are sitting in or the pressure of the floor you are standing on.
4. Now attend to your emotions and thoughts. Again, see how long you can maintain focus without your mind wandering.
5. Now choose an object in your environment and look at it. Focus on this object. Now shift your focus to what is happening around you. Shift back to the object. Can you easily shift focus?

Activities 6.4 and *6.5* will illustrate the importance of your thoughts and begin to get you thinking about how you will direct your thoughts to improve your focus.

Activity 6.4: Quiet Your Mind
For the next minute, think about nothing. Empty your mind of all thoughts.
For thought: How did this work?
Wrap-up: It is impossible to completely empty the mind. However, we do have some control over the thoughts that enter our mind and we can direct those thoughts into positive thoughts by using such mental skills as triggers and releases.

Activity 6.5: Focus On What You Can Do
Picture your competition venue in your mind. See the familiar place you practice or have meets at. Now, the challenge is for you to tell yourself to NOT think about a wild lion standing in the middle of the track infield. Again, do not see the wild lion that escaped from the zoo and is standing in the infield.
For Thought: What did you think about? Chances are you thought about the lion in the infield and what in the world it was doing there!
Wrap-up: What typically happens when you tell yourself not do something like, "do not slow down" or "do not focus on your competition." You think about what you are not supposed to do and often do those things. A more effective strategy is to direct your self-talk so you are telling yourself what to do instead of what not to do.

Learning to understand what you can control is extremely important. Use *Activity 6.6* to help understand the difference between the controllables and uncontrollables.

Activity 6.6: Control the Controllables	
Exercise: In column one is a list of some typical uncontrollables. Add five more uncontrollables to the list. In column two, list things you can control.	
Uncontrollables	**Controllables**
your opponent	attitude
the officiating	effort
temperature (hot-cold)	_____
wind	_____
rain	_____
snow	_____
the schedule	_____
_____	_____
_____	_____
_____	_____
_____	_____

For Thought: Has focusing on uncontrollables gotten you into trouble before?
Wrap-up: Our focus should be on things we can control. However, it is perfectly natural to periodically think about the uncontrollable. Briefly thinking about an uncontrollable is ok, but you should recognize what you are focusing on is an uncontrollable. Use a release technique to forget about the uncontrollable and use cues to immediately return to focus on something you can control at that moment. One thing that you can learn to control is how you choose to react to the uncontrollable. The ability to shift your focus and stay calm under distractors is an important mental skill that needs to be consistently practiced to become automatic.

Table 6.2 provides some examples of cues that could be used during athletic performance.

Table 6.2: Performance Related Cues Example		
Basketball	**Football**	**Baseball or Softball**
Touch	Square	Smooth
Quick	Attack	Contact
Stay low	Explode	Hustle

Use the examples in *Table 6.2* and develop cue words for your event in *Activity 6.7* based upon different skills. Place performance related cue words in your events.

Activity 6.7: Develop Cues for your Event	
Skill	**Cue**

In *Activity 6.8: Distractors*, you are asked to list some possible distractors. Use the distractor examples in column 1 and continue to add to the list in column 2 with additional distractors.

Activity 6.8: Distractors	
Distractors	**Additional Distractors**
Wind	
Rain	
Cold or heat	
Make a turnover	
Fall down	
Officials makes a bad call	
Miss a shot	
Foul or commit a penalty	

A trigger is an action or words that remind you to focus. Triggers are reminders to focus your attention back to the task at hand. Triggers are used to program the proper image. *Activity 6.9: Triggers* lists some triggers that can be used in implementing your mental plan.

Activity 6.9: Triggers	
Some examples of triggers are given in column one. Can you add more triggers to the list in column two that may help you initiate your own mental plan?	
Example Triggers	**Additional Triggers**
Look at the implement	
See the foul pole	
Touch your muscles and think of them as coiled springs	
Clap your hands twice quickly	

A release is a technique that allows you to let go of negative thoughts and feelings that prevent you from concentration on the present.

Use *Activity 6.10: Using Releases* to add to the example of releases you could use.

Activity 6.10: Using Releases	
Some examples of releases are given in column one. Can you add more releases to the list in column two that may help you initiate your own mental plan?	
Release Examples	**More Release Techniques**
Parking-Imagine trouble in your trunk of car	
Grind mistake into ground	
Wipe hand across shirt to wipe mistake away	
Pick up a blade of grass and throw it in the air	
Use flushing toilet movement with your hand	

All athletes will lose focus at some point no matter how well their focus skills. However, what separates great athletes from average athletes is the ability to quickly regain focus after losing it. Mentally strong athletes have a recovery plan to react to the distracting situation. The keys to the recovery plan are called the 3 R's: recognize, relax, re-focus. Use *Table 6.3* and *Activity 6.11* to implement the 3 R's.

Table 6.3: The 3 R's	
Recognize	Recognize you have lost focus and need to regain it.
Relax	Use self-talk and breathing to relax and get back in your proper arousal zone.
Refocus	Re-focus attention on task by using triggers, releases, and cue words.

> **Activity 6.11: Myself After a Mistake**
>
> Think about the last time you made a mistake such as turnover, fouled or missed a shot, committed a penalty or struck out.
>
> When did you recognize you lost focus?
>
> Were you able to relax and get back into the flow of things?
>
> How successful were you in re-focusing?
>
> Now that you know about the signs of being in your proper arousal zone, the components of relaxation, and how to re-focus using cue words, how would you respond in a more positive productive manner?
>
> How would you:
>
> Recognize:
> _____
>
> Relax:
> _____
>
> Refocus:
> _____

Where you put your focus is called a focal point. Focal points can be something you feel, see, or hear. Developing a focal point allows you to place your concentration in a pre-determined place and will help distract you from anything negative that will adversely affect performance.

By developing familiar focal targets, you can consistently increase your focus both before and during your performances. Although we developed several focal points during the activity, I recommend selecting one or two that work for you and develop them.

Use the following activities to help develop your focus skills.

Activity 6.12: Focal Points

Use the examples in column one and then list 4 focal points that you can use in column two in a pre-event situation.

Comment: Because the athletic performance happens quickly, it is difficult to be totally aware of the feeling during the actual flow of performance. Feeling focal points are most often useful before the event, in the pre-performance plan as a tool to stay calm and focused.

Feeling Focal Points Examples:	Feeling Focal points
Feel the stretch of your muscles	1.
Feel your breathing-the air in and out	2.
Feel your feet on the court or field.	3.
Feel the ball or an implement in your hands	4.

Visual Focal Points: Visual focal points are points that you only look at before and during competition to keep in your proper arousal zone. Use the examples in column one and then list 4 visual focal points that you can use in column two in a pre-event situation, then 4 you can use during the event.

Examples	Visual focal points Pre-event	Visual Focal Points During Event
1. Looking at goal line	1.	1.
2. Focus on the court or field	2.	2.
3. See yourself doing your event	3.	3.
4. See yourself stretching	4.	4.

Hearing Focal Points: Listen to only those things that get you in the proper arousal zone and make you feel calm and confident. Use the examples in column one and then list 4 hearing focal points that you can use in column two in a pre-event situation, then 4 you can use during the event.

Examples	Hearing focal points Pre-event	Hearing Focal Points During Event
1. Negative Sounds	1.	1.
2. Others talking about being scared	2.	2.
3.	3.	3.
4.	4.	4.

By developing familiar focal targets, you can consistently increase your focus both before and during your performances. Although we developed several focal points during the activity, I recommend selecting one or two that work for you and develop them.

Use *Activities 6.13* to *6.17* to help develop your focus skills.

Activity 6.13: Focus Cue Development

Phase 1:

You may use a ball or implement for this exercise. Take your shoes or ball or implement and place them five feet away from you. Pick a specific spot on the object to focus your eyes on. Your eyes should stay focused on this spot during the entire exercise.

Place your focus on your breathing. As you inhale, feel the energy coming into your body. Feel your stomach rising. As you exhale, feel the stomach loosen and the tension flow out of your body. When you exhale, repeat a cue word to yourself. This word is your concentration cue and keeps you focused.

Common words that may be used are "strong," "focus," "relax," etc. Whenever you feel your focus start to drift from your visual target, use your breathing and cue word to return your focus on the object.

Continue to focus on the object until you can focus for three minutes without distractions, then move on to phase 2.

Phase 2:

Turn on music but with very low volume at first. Try to stay focused on your spot for the next minute and a half without getting distracted by the music. Whenever you feel your focus start to drift from your visual target, use your breathing and cue word to return your focus on the object.

Continue to focus on the object until you can focus for two minutes without distractions. When you can focus for two-minutes, increase the volume of the music. When you can focus for one minute without losing focus, you are ready for phase 3.

Phase 3:

Place your object directly in front of a TV set. Sit far enough back so that in order for you to still see your object you also see the entire screen. Turn the TV on but with very low volume at first. Try to stay focused on your spot for the next minute and a half without getting distracted by the images on the TV screen. Whenever you feel your focus start to drift from your visual target, use your breathing and cue words to return your focus to the object.

Activity 6.14: Concentration Breathing

Silently say one word related to your sport as you inhale and two words related to your sport as you exhale. See how many breathing cycles you can go through without letting thoughts wander to something else. Set concentration goals.

What caused you to lose concentration?

Activity 6.15: Stick with my Number

Phase 1: Sit quietly with your eyes closed and your feet flat on the floor. Concentrate on your breathing. When you inhale, feel the energy coming into your body and focus on the feeling in your stomach of the air coming in. When you exhale, feel the air going out, and focus on the number one. See the number one in your mind's eye. Repeat "one" in your head, or you can do a combination. Inhale, feel the breath. Exhale, focus on the number one. This is really quite boring, so you'll find your mind wandering. When your mind wonders, recognize that you've lost the proper focus. Return your concentration to your breathing and the feeling of the air coming in. As you exhale, now focus on the number two. See the number two in your mind's eye, repeat the sound "two" in your head, or do a combination. Each time you lose your focus and drift, add a number. Do this exercise for two minutes and see what number you are up to.

Phase 2: Turn on some music and try the same exercise for two minutes.

Activity 6.16: Learn to Maintain Focus

Find a quiet place and choose an object such as a ball or implement. Hold the object in your hands. Get a good sense of how it feels, its texture, color, etc. Put the object down and focus your attention on it. If thoughts wander, bring attention back to the object. Record how long you can maintain your focus on the object. Once you are able to focus for 5 minutes, practice with distractions present. Chart how long you can maintain your attention under these conditions.

Activity 6.17: Concentration Grid Exercise

This exercise helps increase focus and is a fun activity that athletes enjoy participating in.

You will need a pencil and a timer. The concentration grid has numbers from 1 to 99 spread out randomly in the grid.

Go for one minute and see how many numbers you can cross off, starting at 1 and going up in number.

As a means of comparison, people who are able to concentrate effectively and scan well, score in the upper 20's and 30's.

Now for the fun part, have somebody distract you. Start at 99 and work down. The person distracting you can use distracting methods other than hitting you.

10	99	43	71	9	76	61	23	96	90
93	21	97	37	86	17	56	4	66	85
89	8	58	80	49	52	29	42	72	19
15	28	54	38	77	95	34	84	13	26
50	92	70	1	24	30	87	59	100	44
64	45	82	63	91	2	12	68	53	33
75	67	39	27	88	14	83	47	98	62
36	3	31	18	60	35	5	78	11	25
81	57	40	73	48	51	65	41	20	94
46	22	7	79	16	32	6	69	74	55

Table 6.4 is given as an example of a hurdler using cue words while performing a skill.

Table 6.4: Skill Cue Words

Divide your sport into different skills you need to be successful. For each skill, list two to three things that you will focus on during that skill. Then, list one cue word that will bring everything in that skill into focus.

Skill	Main points to focus on	Cue Word (s)
Start to 1st Hurdle	Get to first hurdle without stutter Set rhythm of race Get out of blocks strong Attack first hurdle	BOOM
Clearing Hurdles	Lead leg attacks hurdle Trail leg drives forward	Rhythm
¾ way through race (6th or 7th hurdle)	Fatigue beginning to set in. Look forward to the challenge	Love it!
After last hurdle	Where the race is made Power through final yards	Relax and use power

Using *Table 6.4* as an example, list a skill in your sport in column one and provide Main Points to Focus on and Cue Words.

Activity 6.18: Skill Cue Words

Divide your sport into different skills you need to be successful. For each skill, list two to three things that you will focus on during that skill. Then, list one cue word that will bring everything in that skill into focus.

Skill	Main points to focus on	Cue Word (s)

Chapter 7: Mental Plans

The ultimate use of mental skills is incorporating them into a practice or competition to improve performance. *Table 7.1* provides examples of how you could incorporate mental training into practice.

Table 7.1: Ideas to Incorporate Mental Skills Into a Workout		
Sport	**When to use**	**Mental Activity**
Track and Field	During interval training recovery period	Visualize parts of the upcoming race
Football	After play call	Rapid energization to achieve proper arousal Visualize successful play
Softball	Playing defense before pitch	Use cue words before and during Focus on situation
Baseball	Before pitches when batting	Rapid relaxation or energization Visualize hit
Soccer	During run for ball	Focus on Acceleration Cue words
Volleyball	Before Serve	Rapid relaxation Positive self-talk Focus on process cues
Basketball	Before shooting free throw	Positive self-talk Relaxation- focus on breathing Imagery
Golf	After stroke	Mental recall to review stroke Mental rehearsal to see corrections
Tennis	Before serve	Rapid relaxation Positive self-talk Focus on process cues

Complete *Activity 7.1* and list what you could do to incorporate mental skills into your workouts.

Activity 7.1: Ideas to Incorporate Mental Skills Into a Workout		
Physical Activity in Your Sport	**When to use**	**Mental Activity**

Table 7.2 is an example of how a mental preparation plan could be incorporated into a week. The example of a distance runner is provided as an example to stimulate thinking. Because of the great individualization between athletes and because coaches may have differing training, programs, terminology, plans, etc., use this as a guide. Adapt and adjust as necessary to fit your individual needs and situations.

You will notice in *Table 7.2* under mental practice, a section called "outside of practice." Yes, this is homework. Although mentally skilled athletes incorporate mental skills into actual physical practice, highly mentally skilled athletes go beyond regular practice to further develop their mental skills on their own. I highly encourage you to do your homework. The extra effort will pay off in your ability to use your mental skills automatically when needed.

Table 7.2: Sample Weekly Mental Preparation Plan for a Distance Runner		
Day	Physical Practice	Mental Practice
Monday	1 mile warm-up Dynamic warm-up 4 mile tempo run Static stretch 1 mile jog cool down	Incorporate into practice **Outside of practice:** Review weekly goals Positive self-talk Relaxation Imagery of achieving weekly goals
Tuesday	1 mile warm-up Work on relays	Incorporate into practice **Outside of practice:** Mental recall Affirmations
Wednesday	1 mile warm-up Dynamic warm-up 6 x 100 meter strides 8 x 400 meters with 3 minute rest 1 mile jog cool down	Incorporate into practice **Outside of practice:** Develop competition plan Visualize competition plan
Thursday	1 mile warm-up 20 minutes fartlek Team games Character Building Mental Training	Incorporate into practice **Outside of practice:** Relaxation Visualize competition plan Visualize mental recovery plans
Friday	Competition	See Table 7.3 for example of meet day mental preparation plan
Saturday	Easy recovery jog Stretch	Complete post-competition evaluation Use mental recall to see highlights Use mental recall to see lowlights-rewind to make it a highlight Review previous week goal progress Set new goals with emphasis on process and effort goals
Sunday	Recovery- Walk Bike Swim Stretch	Relaxation Mental rehearsal of next week's goals Positive self-talk Read about a motivating athlete

In *Activity 7.2*, complete the chart indicating what you could do during a week that would develop both the mental and physical components that would lead to a higher performance. Use *Table 7.2* as a guide and adapt to your sport.

Activity 7.2: Design your Weekly Mental Preparation Plan		
Day	Physical Practice	Mental Practice
Monday		Practice: Outside of practice:
Tuesday		Practice: Outside of practice:
Wednesday		Practice: Outside of practice:
Thursday		Practice: Outside of practice:
Friday		Practice: Outside of practice:
Saturday		Outside of practice:
Sunday		Outside of practice:

Once you get to the competition you should have a prepared mental performance plan. *Table 7.3* demonstrates an example mental preparation plan in track and field covering from 80 minutes before competition up to competition time.

Table 7.3: Pre-Competition Mental Preparation Plan		
Time Prior to Start	**Physical WU**	**Mental WU**
75-80 min	Initial check-in Pick-up number Check heat, lane assignments, flight	Relaxation and cue words
65-75 min	Easy jog to get blood flowing	Go over mental performance plan Imagery involving running with perfect form Confidence card or self-talk script Review back-up plans
50-65 min	Stretching	Focus on breathing, relaxation Positive self-talk Quick imagery of portions of event
40-50 min	Dynamic warm-up Good form	Cue words Energization techniques
30-40 min	Drills Proper technique Relax body while doing drills	Positive self-talk Relaxed while doing drills
20-30 min	Strides Specific warm-up to event	Cue words- event specific Increase arousal if needed to get in proper arousal zone Positive mental attitude Focus on personal goals and the processes to make it happen
15-20 min	Bathroom break	Rapid relaxation to deal with pre-race nervousness
10-15 min	Isolation Check final meet gear equipment	Quick review of overall race plan Vividly see running and hitting goal time and splits Use rapid relaxation or energization techniques to get in your proper zone Positive self-talk
10 min	Check-in at event Do final event prep such as starts, strides, final jumps or throws Remove warm-ups React automatically	Maintain proper arousal zone Rapid relaxation Positive self-talk Cue words

Complete the blank form in *Activity 7.3* to develop a mental routine you will use before competition. Use *Table 7.3* as a guide.

Activity 7.3: Pre-Competition Mental Preparation Plan		
Time Prior to Start	**Physical WU**	**Mental WU**

Mental performance plans focus on your goals for practice or competition and are an action plan for achieving them. The focus is on developing specific strategies to maintain a flow mindset during each major phase of your event. *Table 7.4* is an example of a mental performance plan for a hurdler.

Table 7.4: Mental Performance Plan for a Hurdler			
Competition Phase	**Physical**	**Mental**	**Cue Words**
Start to 1st Hurdle	Get to first hurdle without stutter Set rhythm of race Get out of blocks strong Attack first hurdle	Energization out of blocks Focus on power	BOOM Explode Attack
Clearing Hurdles	Lead leg attacks hurdle Trail leg drives forward	Focus on hurdle	Rhythm Smooth
¾ way through race	Fatigue beginning to set in. Look forward to the challenge	Use of cue words Positive self-talk	Love it! Strong Compete

Complete *Activity 7.4* to develop a mental performance plan you can use in competition.

Activity 7.4: Designing Your Mental Performance Plan			
Competition Phase	**Physical**	**Mental**	**Cue Words**

Table 7.5 provides some general guidelines to think about as you develop your mental plans.

Table 7.5: Guidelines to Develop Mental Plans
1. How will you achieve the proper arousal zone for practice or competition?   a. How will you use your relaxation and energization skills to create optimal arousal?   b. What are you goals for practice or competition?   c. What do you want to focus on?   d. Do you have cue words ready?   e. What imagery will you use?
2. How will you develop positive self-talk for practice or competition?

> a. How will you use your positive affirmations and cue words?
> b. How will you use your positive self-talk script?
> c. How will your goals fit into your self-talk?
> d. Will you use imagery to help?
> 3. How will you combine your mental warm-up with your physical warm-up?

Table 7.6 provides examples of mental recovery plans. You should always expect the unexpected. By practicing the unexpected, your automatic response will be a response that will allow you to get your focus back on track.

Table 7.6: Mental Recovery Plan Examples			
Distractors	**Release**	**Re-focus**	**How to prepare for**
Windy day	Exhale air out, blow the wind away	Focus on process goals not outcome Focus on process cues	Practice with a cross wind or occasionally into the wind
Rain	Wipe forehead	Positive self-talk Arousal techniques such as energization	Practice on some rainy days.
Cold	Rub sweats or clothing	Positive self-talk Imagery of goal achievement	Practice in cold
Weather delays	Relaxation breathing	Relaxation Positive self-talk	Start practice and delay it for several minutes
Make mistake	Park mistake in an object	Cue words that focus on process	Simulate recovery from mistakes in practice
Fall down during race	Getting up	Focus on gradually catching up Measure your energy over the remaining distance	In practice, kneeling down and let your teammates get ahead of you and gradually catching up
Turnover or fumble	Flush Toilet	Relaxation Positive self-talk Imagery of next event	Simulate regaining composure in practice
Strikeout	See foul pole	Relaxation Focus on next task	Shift focus to support team, playing defense
Technique is off with little rhythm	Play music in head	Focus on relaxation Process cue words	Use energization or relaxation techniques to get into proper arousal zone

Complete *Activity 7.5* to develop your mental recovery plans to help you recover and refocus.

Activity 7.5: Your Mental Recovery Plan			
Distractors	Release	Re-focus	How to prepare for

Use *Activity 7.6* as a way to assess and evaluate where you are at. What are you doing well? What do you need to work on?

Activity 7.6: Post Competition Evaluation	
Name of competition: _____ Date: _____	
Pre-competition meal:	
_____	
Pre-competition mental training:	
_____	
Rate the following on a scale of 1-10 (10 being high)	
Your overall performance	_____
Warm-up	_____
Use of mental training before event	_____
Use of mental training competition plan	_____
Use of mental recovery plan	_____
Start	_____
Middle of event	_____
End of event	_____
Encouraging teammates	_____
Proper nutrition	_____
Proper hydration	_____
Challenged myself	_____
Accomplished competition plan	_____
Things I did well 1._____ 2._____	

Things I contributed to the team
1._____
2._____
Things I need to work on
1._____
2._____

Resources

Burton, D., & Raedeke, T. (2008). *Sport psychology for coaches*. Champaign, IL: Human Kinetics.

Feltz D., & Landers, M. (2007). The effects of mental practice on motor skill learning and performance: A meta-analysis. *Journal of Sport Psychology, 5.*

Freeman, W. (2014). *Track and field coaching essentials, USA Track and Field.* Champaign, IL: Human Kinetics.

Goldberg, A. (2012). *Using your head for championship performance in track and field.* Amazon Digital Services.

Gilbert, J. (2011). Teaching sport psychology to high school student-athletes: The psychological uniform and the game plan format. *Journal of Sport Psychology in Action, 2.*

Hammermeister, J. (2010). *Cornerstones of coaching, the building blocks of success for sport coaches and teams.* Traverse City, MI: Cooper Publishing, Co.

Hogg, J. (1997). *Mental skills for young athletes.* Edmonton, Alberta, Canada: Sport Excel Publishing Inc.

Janssen, J., & Candrea, M. (1994). *Mental toughness training for softball: A guide and workbook for athletes and coaches.* Casa Grande, AZ: Southwest Campus Publications.

Lefkowits, J., & McDuff, D. (n.d.). Mental toughness training manual for baseball/softball players.

Johnson, D. (2012). *Wrestling drills for the mat and mind.* Ithaca, NY: MAG, Incorporated.

Judge, L., Bell, R., Bellar, D., & Wanless. E. (2010). Developing a mental game plan: Mental periodization for achieving a "flow" state for track and field throws athlete. *The Sport Journal, 13(4).*

Murphy, S. (1994). Imagery interventions in sport. *Medicine Science Sports Exercise 26(4).*

Murphy, S., & Martin, K. A. (2002). The use of imagery in sport. In T. Horn (Ed.), *Advances in sport psychology* (2 ed., pp. 405-439). Champaign, IL: Human Kinetics.

Nideffer, R. M. (1989). Psychological services for the U.S. track and field team. *The Sport Psychologist, 3.*

Orlick, T., & Partington, J. (1988). Mental links to excellence. *The Sport Psychologist, 2.*

Reardon, J., & Gordin, R. (1999). Psychological skill development leading to a peak performance "flow state". *Track and Field Coaches Review, 3(2).*

Porter, K. (2003). *The mental athlete*. Champaign, IL: Human Kinetics.

Risk, B. (2009). *Periodized sport psychology-Building the bulletproof athlete.* Fairport, NY: Glass Dragon Digital Publishing.

Rockwood, D. (2011). *Closing the gap: Applied sport psychology for high school.* Provo, UT: Rockwood Publishing.

Smith, D. (1999). *Make success measurable: A mindbook-workbook for setting goals and taking action.* Toronto, Ontario, Canada: John Wiley and Sons, Inc.

Stanbrough, M. (2012). *Mental skills and drills for track and field.* Emporia, KS: Roho Publishing.

Stanbrough, M. (2012). *Motivational moments in men's track and field.* Emporia, KS: Roho Publishing.

Townsend, D. (2005). *Mind training for swimmers.* Jamul, CA: Belissima Publishing.

Vealey, R. (2005). *Coaching for the inner edge.* Morgantown, WV: Fitness Information Technology.

Vernachchia, R., & Statler, T. (2005). *The psychology of high performance track and field.* Mountain View, CA: TAFnews Press

Visek, A., Harris, B., & Blom, L. (2013). Mental training with youth sport teams: Developmental considerations and best-practice recommendations. *Journal of Sport Psychology in Action, 4.*

Wann, D., & Church, B. (1998). A method for enhancing the psychological skills of track and field athletes. *Track Coach, (4).*

Weinberg, R., & Gould, D. (2006). *Foundations of sport and exercise psychology* (4th ed.). Champaign, IL: Human Kinetics.

Weintraub, A. (2009). *Coaches guide to winning the mental game.* Monterey, CA: Coaches Choice.

Woolfolk, R., Parrish, M., & Murphy. (1985). The effects of positive and negative imagery on motor skill performance. *Cognitive Therapy and Research, 9.*

About the Author

Dr. Mark Stanbrough has over thirty years' experience of successfully teaching mental skills to students and coaches and has coaching experience at the collegiate, high school, middle school and club levels. He is a professor in the Department of Health, Physical Education and Recreation at Emporia State University in Kansas and is the director of Coaching Education. The Coaching Education program at Emporia State is currently one of only ten universities in the United State to be accredited by the National Council for the Accreditation of Coaching Education. He teaches graduate and undergraduate exercise physiology and sports psychology classes. He was a co-founder of the online physical education graduate program, the first in United States to go completely online.

He received his Ph.D. in exercise physiology from the University of Oregon, and undergraduate and master's degrees from Emporia State in physical education. He has served as department chair and has served on the National Association for Sport and Physical Education National Sport Steering Committee and is a past member of the board of directors for the National Council for the Accreditation of Coaching Education.

Coach Stanbrough served eight years as the head men's and women's cross country/track and field coach at Emporia State (1984-1992) with the 1986 women's cross country team finishing second at the NAIA national meet. He has also coached at Emporia High School and Glasco High School in Kansas. He competed in cross country and track and field for the Emporia State Hornets and has been inducted as a member of the Emporia State University Athletic Hall of Honor. He has also been inducted into the Emporia State Health, Physical Education, Recreation Hall of Honor and has won numerous coach-of-the-year awards at the high school and collegiate levels.

www.ingramcontent.com/pod-product-compliance
Lightning Source LLC
LaVergne TN
LVHW051849080426
835512LV00018B/3148